TEACHING
SWIMMING

Steps to Success

David G. Thomas, MS
Professor Emeritus
State University of New York–Binghamton

Leisure Press
Champaign, Illinois

Library of Congress Cataloging-in-Publication Data

Thomas, David G., 1924-
    Teaching swimming.

    (Steps to success activity series)
    Bibliography: p.
    1. Swimming—Study and teaching.   I. Title.
II. Series.
GV836.35.T48 1989   797.2′1   87-35285
ISBN 0-88011-310-3

Developmental Editor: Judy Patterson Wright, PhD
Production Director: Ernie Noa
Copy Editor: Peter Nelson
Assistant Editors: Kathy Kane and Julie Anderson
Proofreader: Laurie McGee
Typesetter: Yvonne Winsor
Text Design: Keith Blomberg
Text Layout: Gordon Cohen
Cover Design: Jack Davis
Cover Photo: Bill Morrow
Illustrations By: Tim Offenstein
Printed By: Phillips Brothers Printers

ISBN: 0-88011-310-3

Printed in the United States of America

10 9 8 7 6 5 4 3 2 1

Leisure Press
A Division of Human Kinetics Publishers, Inc.
Box 5076, Champaign, IL 61820
1-800-342-5457
1-800-334-3665 (in Illinois)

Contents

Series Preface

The Steps to Success Activity Series is a breakthrough in skill instruction through the development of complete learning progressions—the *steps to success*. These *steps* help students quickly perform basic skills successfully and prepare them to acquire advanced skills readily. At each step, students are encouraged to learn at their own pace and to integrate their new skills into the total action of the activity, which motivates them to achieve.

The unique features of the Steps to Success Activity Series are the result of comprehensive development—through analyzing existing activity books, incorporating the latest research from the sport sciences and consulting with students, instructors, teacher educators, and administrators. This groundwork pointed up the need for three different types of books—for participants, instructors, and teacher educators—which we have created and together comprise the Steps to Success Activity Series.

The *participant book* for each activity is a self-paced, step-by-step guide; learners can use it as a primary resource for a beginning activity class or as a self-instructional guide. The unique features of each *step* in the participant book include

- sequential illustrations that clearly show proper technique for all basic skills,
- helpful suggestions for detecting and correcting errors,
- excellent drill progressions with accompanying *Success Goals* for measuring performance, and
- a complete checklist for each basic skill for a trained observer to rate the learner's technique.

A comprehensive *instructor guide* accompanies the participant's book for each activity, emphasizing how to individualize instruction. Each *step* of the instructor's guide promotes successful teaching and learning with

- teaching cues (*Keys to Success*) that emphasize fluidity, rhythm, and wholeness,

- criterion-referenced rating charts for evaluating a participant's initial skill level,
- suggestions for observing and correcting typical errors,
- tips for group management and safety,
- ideas for adapting every drill to increase or decrease the difficulty level,
- quantitative evaluations for all drills (*Success Goals*), and
- a complete test bank of written questions.

The series textbook, *Instructional Design for Teaching Physical Activities*, explains the *steps to success* model, which is the basis for the Steps to Success Activity Series. Teacher educators can use this text in their professional preparation classes to help future teachers and coaches learn how to design effective physical activity programs in school, recreation, or community teaching and coaching settings.

After identifying the need for participant, instructor, and teacher educator texts, we refined the *steps to success* instructional design model and developed prototypes for the participant and the instructor books. Once these prototypes were fine-tuned, we carefully selected authors for the activities who were not only thoroughly familiar with their sports but had years of experience in teaching them. Each author had to be known as a gifted instructor who understands the teaching of sport so thoroughly that he or she could readily apply the *steps to success* model.

Next, all of the participant and instructor manuscripts were carefully developed to meet the guidelines of the *steps to success* model. Then our production team, along with outstanding artists, created a highly visual, user-friendly series of books.

The result: The Steps to Success Activity Series is the premier sports instructional series available today. The participant books are the best available for helping you to become a master player, the instructor guides will help you to become a master teacher, and the teacher educator's text prepares you to design your own programs.

This series would not have been possible without the contributions of the following:

- Dr. Joan Vickers, instructional design expert,
- Dr. Rainer Martens, Publisher,
- the staff of Human Kinetics Publishers, and

- the *many* students, teachers, coaches, consultants, teacher educators, specialists, and administrators who shared their ideas—and dreams.

Judy Patterson Wright
Series Editor

Preface

Teaching Swimming: Steps to Success was written for two groups of teachers: (a) those who are experienced, but have not closed their minds to innovation and are seeking methods beyond the traditional, and (b) those who are just starting out on their own or, perhaps, are graduate assistants assigned to teach beginner swimming.

The first group will recognize the value of this text just by leafing through it, looking at the steps, drills, goals, and evaluation criteria. The second group will breathe a sigh of relief and exclaim, ''Wow! This is just what I need to guide me in class organization and help me learn to conduct class drills.'' I know! I wish such a book had existed when I came into teaching with lots of theory and little practical experience. That's the purpose of this book—to put a *practical* tool in the hands of the teacher who is looking for new ideas or help in getting started.

Upon my retirement as professor of physical education at the State University of New York, Binghamton, I met Dr. Rainer Martens and Dr. Judy Patterson Wright of Human Kinetics Publishers and Leisure Press. These two remarkable people were working on a series of sports activity texts based on the scholarly research concepts of Dr. Joan Vickers. Our interests merged and they guided me in putting my practical knowledge into a truly unique form, incorporating all the theoretical research. *Teaching Swimming: Steps to Success* is unique because it is research-based and totally useable.

My profound thanks to those already mentioned and to the remarkable artists who illustrated my concepts, and to the copy editor who sifted my syntax and made it understandable.

The person who reads and uses this book has in hand the information necessary to save many lives and, at the same time, to introduce people to a lifetime sport that can be enjoyed to the age of 90 and beyond. If using this book starts one person on a career as rewarding as mine has been, I will feel fully compensated.

David G. Thomas

Implementing the Steps to Success Staircase

This book is meant to be flexible not only to your students' needs but to your needs as well. It is common to hear that students' perceptions of a task change as the task is learned. However, we often forget that teachers' perceptions and actions also change (Goc-Karp & Zakrajsek, 1987; Housner & Griffey, 1985; Imwold & Hoffman, 1983).

More experienced or master teachers tend to approach the teaching of activities in a similar manner. They are highly organized (e.g., they do not waste time getting groups together or use long explanations); they integrate information (e.g., from biomechanics, kinesiology, exercise physiology, motor learning, sport psychology, cognitive psychology, instructional design, etc.); and they relate basic skills into the larger game or performance context. This includes succinctly explaining why the basic skills, concepts, or tactics are important within the game or performance setting. Then, usually within a few minutes, their students are placed into practice situations that progress in steps that follow logical manipulations of factors such as:

- depth of the water,
- time,
- distance, and
- the addition or removal of equipment.

This book will show you how the basic swimming skills and selected physiological, psychological, and other pertinent knowledge are interrelated (see Appendix A for an overview). You can use this information not only to gain insights into the various interrelationships but also to define the subject matter for swimming. The following questions offer specific suggestions for implementing this knowledge base and help you to evaluate and improve your teaching methods, which include class organization, drills, objectives, progressions, and evaluations.

1. Under what conditions do you teach?
   - How much space is available?
   - What type of equipment is available?
   - What is the average class size?
   - How much time is allotted per class session?
   - Do you have any teaching assistants?

2. What are your students' initial skill levels?
   - Look for the rating charts located in the beginning of most steps (chapters) to identify the criteria that discriminate between beginning, novice, and accomplished skill levels.

3. What is the best order to teach swimming skills?
   - Follow the sequence of steps (chapters) used in this book.
   - See Appendix B.1 for suggestions on when to introduce, review, or continue practicing each step.
   - Based on your answers to the previous questions, use the form in Appendix B.2 to order the steps that you will be able to cover in the time available.

4. What objectives do you want your students to accomplish by the end of a lesson, unit, or course?
   - For your technique or qualitative objectives, select from the Keys to Success and/or the Keys to Success Checklists that are provided for all basic skills.
   - For your performance or quantitative objectives, select from the Success Goals provided for each drill.
   - For written questions on safety, rules, technique, history, and psychological aspects of swimming, select from the Test Bank of written questions.
   - See the Sample Individual Program (Appendix C.1) for selected technique and performance objectives for a 16-week unit.

- For unit objectives, adjust your total number of selected objectives to fit your unit length (use the form in Appendix C.2).
- For organizing daily objectives, see the Sample Lesson Plan in Appendix D.1, and modify the basic lesson plan form in Appendix D.2 to best fit your needs.

5. How will you evaluate your students?

- Read the section on Evaluation Ideas.
- Decide on your type of grading system, for example, letter grades, pass–fail, total points, percentages, skill levels (bronze, silver, gold), and so forth.

6. Which activities should be selected to achieve student objectives?

- Follow the drills and/or exercises for each step because they are specifically designed for large groups of students and are presented in a planned, easy-to-difficult order. Avoid a random approach to selecting drills and exercises.
- Modify drills as necessary to best fit your students' skill levels by following the suggestions for decreasing and increasing the difficulty level of each drill.

- Ask students to meet the Success Goal listed for each drill.
- Use the cross-reference to the corresponding step and drill number within the participants' book, *Swimming: Steps to Success*, for class assignments or makeups.

7. What rules and expectations do you have for your class?

- For general management and safety guidelines, read the section "Preparing Your Class for Success."
- For specific guidelines, read the section "Group Management and Safety Tips" included with each drill.
- Let your students know what your rules are during your class orientation and/or first day of class. Then post them and repeat them often.

Teaching is a complex task, requiring you to make many decisions that will affect both you and your students (see Figure 1). Use this book to create an effective and successful learning experience for you and everyone you teach. And remember, have fun too!

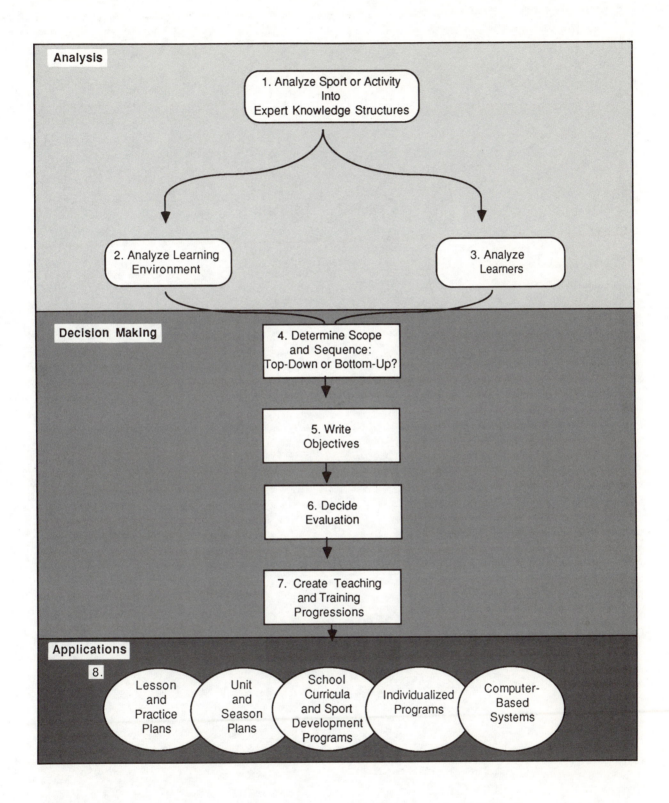

Figure 1 Instructional design model utilizing expert knowledge structures. *Note.* From *Instructional Design for Teaching Physical Activities* by J.N. Vickers, in press, Champaign, IL: Human Kinetics. Copyright by Joan N. Vickers. Reprinted by permission. This instructional design model has appeared in earlier forms in *Badminton: A Structures of Knowledge Approach* (p. 1) by J.N. Vickers and D. Brecht, 1987, Calgary AB: University Printing Services. Copyright 1987 by Joan N. Vickers; and ''The Role of Expert Knowledge Structures in an Instructional Design Model for Physical Education'' by J.N. Vickers, 1983, *Journal of Teaching in Physical Education,* **2**(3), p. 20. Copyright 1983 by Joan N. Vickers.

Preparing Your Class for Success

Before you begin teaching your class, you need to make many procedural decisions. Use the following items for creating an effective learning environment.

GENERAL CLASS MANAGEMENT

Students should be given guidance as to their actions when they enter the pool area. They should know that they should never enter the water until the instructor tells them to do so. Rather, they should sit in an assigned area or begin warm-up exercises upon entering the pool area.

General pool rules must be explained, such as these following:

1. The Health Department requires all bathers to take a shower with hot, soapy water before entering the pool.
2. Walk, don't run, on the deck.
3. Swimming in the diving area is prohibited. (Explain.)
4. Diving into shallow areas is prohibited. (Explain.)
5. Students wearing metal pins or clips in their hair must wear a cap. (Pins and clips invariably come loose. Metal ones make rust marks that are hard to clean. All-plastic barrettes or elastic ponytail ties are okay.)
6. For safety, long hair must be tied back (or a cap worn) to keep it out of eyes and mouth.
7. Use of the diving boards is limited to one person at a time, and divers must exit the pool without swimming in front of another board.

Rules on attendance, various types of absences that are or are not allowable, grading policies, and acceptable attire in class must be explained. Explain the policy on towel acquisition and disposal, unless students are required to bring their own. Are notebooks and textbooks allowed or required, and should they be brought to class? What written tests will be given when, and what will they cover? What procedure is followed in the event of a fire drill while swimmers are in the pool?

CLASS ORGANIZATION TECHNIQUES

Water temperatures of 82-84 °F are recommended for teaching beginner classes, but students still become chilled after 30 to 40 minutes in the water. They will become chilled even more rapidly if they are in and out of the water frequently during the class. We know that a short demonstration should be followed immediately by practice of the skill. In swimming, though, it is sometimes best to demonstrate all skills to be covered while the students are still dry and warm; then the students can do them all during one time in the water. Each skill or set of skills must be evaluated with the comfort of the student in mind. No student learns as much when shivering from the cold.

A whistle is a must in swimming classes because the acoustics in swimming pools are notoriously bad. It is imperative that you be able to get the attention of the class instantly, even when many ears are underwater or the noise level approaches bedlam.

Arrange your class around a corner whenever possible to allow all to see and hear better. Get the students up onto the side to watch demonstrations in the water. Your presence in the water is extremely important to the students when teaching very basic skills in which fear is a factor. However, for advanced skills you can see and correct the students better from the elevated side or deck.

In a class situation, many basic skill drills must be done on an individual basis for safety. As soon as safety allows, a "stagger drill" is usually most efficient, because it allows individual attention but minimizes the time needed for each student. "Wave drills" are most efficient to maximize the practice time each student gets, but individual attention is sacrificed.

A stagger drill is one in which the class is lined up along the side or end wall of the pool and each student starts the drill individually on command. The commands are given at intervals such that the first student is only partway through the skill when the next student starts. Continuing in this manner, an across-pool drill would result in the students being in a staggered line across the pool; thus the name *stagger* drill.

A wave drill is organized by having the students, in line, count off by threes, fours, or whatever number the instructor wishes, to limit the number of students in each wave. Then, on command all the number ones begin the drill simultaneously in a wave composed of one third, or one fourth, and so on, of the class. The second wave (of "twos") follows when the first wave is partway through the skill. Then the third wave follows, and so on, resulting in a series of "waves" of students performing the skill at discrete intervals. This type of drill allows each student space to perform when the class is too large for all to perform at once. The term *mass drill* refers to a drill in which the entire class begins at the same time.

CLASS WARM-UP DRILLS

Learning is enhanced, and comfort is increased, when a class is made ready for physical exertion by proper warm-up activities. Warm-up activity should not be a waste of time but should encompass some form of movement that prepares the body and enhances a skill at the same time.

Stretching and breathing exercises are valuable to swimming classes prior to entering the water, and vigorous skill drills may be used to acclimate the student to the temperature of the water immediately after entry. Breathing and stretching exercises are listed in the participant's book under the heading "Preparing Your Body For Success." These are excellent and sufficient, but you may wish to add variety to your warm-ups with the following:

Stretching

1. **Ankle Stretch**

   Propulsion from a flutter kick is dependent upon the flexibility of the ankle. Kneel on a mat on both knees with toes pointed. Very gently sit back on your heels until you can feel tension in the ankles. Hold the position for 5 seconds and rock forward again. Repeat 4 times.

2. **Achilles Stretch**

   Stand facing a wall, about arm's length away, arms outstretched, hands against the wall. Keep your heels flat against the floor as you slowly bend your elbows, allowing your body to lean toward the wall. Feel the stretch in the back of your legs. Repeat 4 times. (Very supple persons may start with the toes up on a 1-inch board.)

3. **Shoulder Stretch**

   An overhand swimming stroke requires flexible shoulders. Hold your towel by opposite corners in front of you. Maintain your hold as you raise the towel above your head and try to bring it down behind you. Then bring it back overhead to the front again. Repeat 4 times. (If your shoulders are very supple, shorten your grip on the towel until you feel tension in the shoulders. If your shoulders are very tight, bend an elbow as needed to get the towel behind you.)

Water Warm-Ups

1. **Running**

   In water 3-5 feet deep, run as fast as possible across the pool, using your hands as aids to pull you along. (This teaches both the effects of water resistance and adjustment to motion in the more dense medium.)

2. **Jumping**

   In chest-deep water, jump as high as you can repeatedly from both feet. Continue for 2 minutes, bounding forward through the water. (This teaches balance and the buoyant effect of the water.)

3. **Bobbing**

   In chest-deep water, sink under while exhaling through your mouth, or mouth and nose. Rise and inhale through your mouth. Press with both arms while rising and lift with both arms while submerging. Continue bobbing and move about the area. Breathe normally and take smaller breaths if you feel light-headed. This is an excellent drill for teaching rhythmic breathing, and should be practiced often (see Step 10, Drill 1).

4. Kicking

Becoming acclimated to the water temperature can be combined with skill practice. Holding a kickboard at arm's length, float prone in the water and kick across the pool. Beginners should use a bent-knee kick; as the skills improve, a crawl kick should be substituted. Count the kicks in groups of 6. Exhale for 3 counts with your face in the water, then raise your chin and inhale on 3 counts.

5. Follow the Leader

In single file, jump across the pool in chest-deep water. Try to catch and hold the rhythm of the leader, so everyone is jumping at the same time.

6. Follow-the-Leader Bobbing

Repeat Drill 5, but sink under on each jump and exhale underwater. Thus, go "bobbing" across the pool. Keep the sinking and rising rhythm smooth. Adapt your breathing rhythm to that of the leader.

TAPER DRILLS

Because of the water temperature, it is unlikely that swimmers need cool-down drills at the end of a session. However, some sort of fun activity is recommended to finish the session in a relaxed manner. The following games provide a 5-minute taper-off period that is fun to do.

1. Double Water Ball

This game is quickly organized and uses little equipment. It can run for any time period. Rules are minimal.

Equipment: Two balls (about the size of water polo balls or 12- to 15-inch beach balls, preferably of different colors), caps for one team, and a whistle. Play in water

of standing depth. Pool sides or float-lines mark boundaries. Any size area may be used.

The Game: Two teams (any number of swimmers on each) line up on opposite sides of the area. Each team has one ball. At the whistle each team tries to maintain control of the ball they hold and to gain possession of the other ball. A point is scored when one player holds both balls in contact with each other for a period of 3 seconds.

Rules: Balls must be kept above the water. Players play only for the ball—they may not grab or hold another player, but they may attack the ball. If two players are tied up over one ball, the whistle blows, the other ball remaining in play, and the contested ball is thrown into the middle of the court. If a ball goes out of bounds, it is thrown up near the spot where it went out (the other ball remaining in play). When a point is scored, one ball is given to an opposing team member at a point remote from the other ball. If a ball is taken underwater, it is thrown up in midcourt. A player caught holding another must sit out until a point is scored. Make up any other rules you wish.

2. Modified Water Polo

This game is quickly organized and uses minimal equipment. It is recommended that a lightweight beach ball be used, because a water polo ball is hard and heavy and players tend to throw too hard.

Equipment: One 12- to 15-inch beach ball, caps for one team, four kickboards, and a whistle. Preparation: Play in water of standing depth. Make a goal on the deck of each side of the pool about 6 inches back from the edge: Stand one kickboard on edge facing the pool and lean it against another kickboard standing on edge at right angles; they should be easily knocked over.

The Game: Teams (any number of swimmers) line up on opposite sides of the pool. At the whistle, the ball is thrown into the center of the area. Players try to throw the ball to knock over the goal defended by the other team. Players may not strike or hold an opponent. Balls thrown out of bounds (including unsuccessful goal shots) are awarded to the opposing team at that spot. Penalty for rules violations: removal from the game until a goal is scored. Time for the game: whatever the referee decides. Make more rules as needed.

3. King of the Kickboard

Each student gets a kickboard and with some difficulty can learn to stand on it in shallow water. When all are standing on kickboards, at a signal each tries to push the others off their kickboards. Students can move around by stooping to chin depth, which allows them to lift their feet momentarily and propel themselves with their arms. The last student remaining on his or her kickboard wins. Otherwise, pair each student with another in head-to-head competition and have a winner in each pair.

Variation: Students hold kickboards between their legs and float around the pool, propelling themselves with their arms. Each tries to unseat the others. Any part of any kickboard that breaks the water surface disqualifies the rider.

4. Trick of the Day

Not a contest, but a fun thing to try. Each student gets two kickboards and tries while floating vertically (in water 5 feet deep) to put one kickboard under each foot.

EQUIPMENT

Fortunately, swimming classes require very little equipment for teaching. The items listed for this course are usually found at all pools, or may be made very quickly, easily, and inexpensively.

1. Kickboard

This is a flat piece of plastic foam, 1 inch thick and about 22 inches × 12 inches. Usually one end is rounded.

Quantity: One per student.

2. Leg Float

Several different designs are available, but most consist of two cylinders of plastic foam about 4 inches in diameter and 6 inches long held together by a cord woven through the cylinders.

Quantity: One per student.

3. Deep Float Leg Support

Make these yourselves by using a 1/2-gallon plastic jug with handle. Tie a piece of string to the handle so a loop 4 inches in diameter hangs 12-15 inches below the jug.

Quantity: One per student.

4. Float Belt

This can best be made by using a 2-inch woven nylon belt with a quick-release buckle or a D-ring buckle (scuba weight belts are ideal). Cut plastic foam blocks that are about 2 inches square and 6 inches long. Slit the blocks so the belt can be threaded through them. Each belt will require from two to six blocks. Have some spare blocks available.

Quantity: Probably three will be enough for a class. They are used only by those who are not buoyant enough to float motionless.

5. Mask and Snorkel Set

Standard scuba masks and snorkels are expensive and are personal-fit items. Students may be asked to bring their own, or several sets of varying styles and sizes may be furnished. It is possible, but not nearly as effective, to use snorkels only. The cost for snorkels alone is small enough to require one per student. An elastic headband is required to hold the snorkel upright if masks are not used.

Quantity: Ideally, one set per student, but 5 sets of varying style and size may be used alternately by a class of ten to twelve.

6. Swim Fins

Helpful but not essential. They are expensive, and several sizes would be needed to fit all students.

Quantity: Ideally, one pair per student in the proper size. One pair in each of four sizes could be shared by a class of ten to twelve.

7. Hula Hoop

This is a ring of rigid, 1-inch plastic tubing about 36 inches in diameter (40-inch diameter is preferred). The point where the ends are joined must be plugged solidly and perhaps coated to make the joint waterproof. The ring must float, but a small weight must be tied to one point to make the ring stand vertically on the bottom of the pool. Some models are not tubular but may be used so long as the plastic floats.

Quantity: Three or four are enough for an entire class. It is possible to use only one for the class, but more are fun and can be adapted for use in many innovative games. They are not specified for use until the diving skills are taught (Step 22).

8. Diving Rings

This is a small ring about 4-6 inches in diameter, made of hard rubber or some other material that sinks. Any small object that sinks and can be held under one foot may be substituted. They are used as objects for retrieval when teaching the prone float.

Quantity: Ideally, one per student, but one for every three or four students can suffice.

9. 10-Pound Brick

This is the rubber-covered brick that is usually used in teaching lifesaving classes. Most pools have several for use in recreation and instruction. They are not essential to this course and are suggested for use in only one drill (Step 21, Drill 4).

Quantity: Four or five would be ideal, but the drill can be conducted with one or two.

10. Goggles

The water in many pools causes eye irritation. Students should be allowed to wear small goggles that cover only the eyes at any time they wish. They are not a part of the instructional equipment but add to comfort and enjoyment. Insist on sessions without goggles occasionally so the students do not become dependent on them.

EQUIPMENT PREPARATION

You must plan each day's lesson in advance so that the equipment needed for the day can be assembled and set out. Equipment should always be readily available, to avoid wasting time. Students should select masks, snorkels, and/or fins prior to class on days when they will be used, to avoid having to select proper-sized gear during class time.

ESSENTIAL EQUIPMENT

The list below designates equipment that is absolutely essential for protection of the students and for avoiding liability for negligence in case of an accident.

1. Highly visible depth markers around the perimeter of the water area
2. Reaching poles and/or shepherds' crooks near deep-water areas
3. Ring buoys with 60 feet of line attached, placed around the deep-water area
4. Rescue tubes placed at intervals near the water's edge
5. Float lines separating deep from shallow areas and (for open-water areas) marking the boundaries of the swimming areas
6. An adequate first aid kit, frequently checked and stocked, located conspicuously nearby
7. Emergency phone numbers placed prominently at the nearest phone
8. Highly visible warning signs (especially "no-diving" signs) placed strategically at all danger areas

SAFETY

Entering the water carries with it an inherent risk. You must deal every day with the possibility of a momentary lapse of concentration or vigilance that could easily lead to the death of a student. Safety precautions must be carefully drawn and scrupulously observed. Furthermore, in today's lawsuit-mad society, your own financial safety is as much at stake as your students' physical safety. SAFETY IS YOUR PRIMARY CONCERN—your safety and the students'.

Safety Rules

Recommended safety rules for swimming classes are listed below.

1. Check daily before class to ascertain that all rescue equipment is in its proper place and in operable condition.
2. Arrange for a person properly qualified in lifeguarding to be present during all swimming classes in addition to the instructors. Assign that person the sole duty of guarding the overall situation without having additional, distracting duties.
3. Allow no students to enter the pool *area* prior to the arrival of the instructor, unless a qualified lifeguard is on duty. No student should enter the *water* prior to the instructor's arrival.
4. For your own peace of mind, walk completely around the pool at the end of each class period, checking for objects on the bottom. If a body is discovered at a later time, you will know it was not because of your oversight.
5. Post and maintain written emergency procedures. Be sure all participants are aware of them.
6. Mark water depths prominently. Be sure all students are aware of the depths at all points in the pool before classes begin. A "depth line" on the wall of the pool is an excellent device. This is a line painted on the wall of the natatorium at a height above the deck corresponding to the depth of the water at that point.
7. Familiarize your students with the general area rules, such as pertain to running, no-diving areas, horseplay, and so on.

Pre-Class Checklist

Effective teaching requires attention to creating the best learning environment possible within the given circumstances. It requires you, the instructor, to anticipate circumstances that may arise and to do everything possible to minimize the effects of unforseen circumstances on the class situation.

A few things to which attention must be given prior to class time are listed below:

- Check to see that all locker rooms are unlocked and all lights are on.
- Check to see that all safety equipment is in place and ready for use.
- Check the water temperature and be sure all water tests have been taken and recorded.
- Check that mats, other exercise equipment, and the exercise area are ready for pre-class warm-up.
- Double-check that all class lists, progress charts, and attendance charts are at hand.
- Do you have a whistle?
- Prepare all teaching equipment.
- Make sure that your nonteaching lifeguard is present.
- Sit for a minute and mentally review your lesson plan for the day. Take a deep breath and greet your class with a smile and great enthusiasm.

Liability Checklist

Protecting yourself and your institution against liability lawsuits requires that your students know, understand, and appreciate the risks of the activities in which they are engaged. It is not enough to warn of dangers by signs—you must also explain the possible consequences of disobeying the signs. It is probably best to draw up a written statement of risks and consequences to give to each student. A written list avoids the possibility of your forgetting to mention one or more parts in an oral presentation. An example of a written warning list for a swimming class is shown in Table 1.

Instructors should keep such signed warnings on file for at least 5 years. Waivers of liability and legal release statements are of some

Table 1 Warning of Risks Involved in Swimming

Swimming, because it requires entry into the water, encompasses some inherent risks, the most obvious of which is drowning. Instructors in this class are fully qualified lifesavers and are trained in methods for prevention of aquatic accidents. Nevertheless, failure to abide by the rules of conduct of the swimming area or to follow the instructions given by those in charge could result in ingestion of water into the lungs, causing pneumonia, suffocation, or death by drowning. Failure to obey posted rules of conduct for the area and in regard to entering the water could result in such serious spinal injuries as a broken neck, paralysis, paraplegia, or quadriplegia.

I have read the statement above. It has been explained to my satisfaction, and I am fully cognizant of the risks involved in this class.

(signed) _____ Date _____

_____

value in protecting an instructor from liability also, but instructors should **not** rely on them for assured protection.

NINE LEGAL DUTIES

There are nine legal duties owed by an instructor to the students of a course to fulfill the obligation of liability. We list them here as they apply to a swimming course.

1. Adequate Supervision

As an instructor, you must provide adequate supervision to protect students from inherent or extraneous hazards of the situation.

2. Sound Planning

You must also provide good, sound planning for the activities being conducted. Sound progressions are especially important in swimming, where attempting advanced skills without proper basic preparation could result in serious consequences.

3. Inherent Risks

We have already mentioned the inherent risks involved in swimming. You have a duty to the students to warn them adequately of such risks and to be sure they understand the risks.

4. Safe Swimming Environment

You must provide a swimming area that is free of hidden or unmarked hazards. A safe environment also includes the surrounding area and the safety and rescue equipment available. You are expected to inspect the facility and equipment regularly and thoroughly.

5. Evaluating Students' Fitness for the Activity

You must evaluate your students' injuries or handicaps and determine to what extent such disabilities may limit their safe participation. You must also attempt to ascertain the mental attitudes of students where such attitudes may become a hazard to their safety. Fear may be a real handicap that can limit participation in swimming.

6. Matching or Equating Students

When students are paired for participation in a drill, you must be sure that each of the pair can perform all of the skills you require of them both. A novice should not be expected to keep up with, or protect from harm, an advanced swimmer assigned as a partner.

7. Emergency First Aid Procedures

In the event of an accident, you must be prepared to provide adequate medical assistance. It is your duty to your students to have planned and posted medical procedures that can be put immediately into action. Failure to provide this protection can result in court findings of negligence.

8. Other Legal Concerns

You cannot restrict your classes or your students in such a way as to violate their civil rights. Your legal duty is to provide for the legal rights and concerns of your students, staff, and any spectators allowed during the program.

9. General Legal Concerns

In today's lawsuit-happy environment, you must be aware of all the possibilities for liability and must take adequate measures to protect yourself. Always keep accurate records of your activities, especially in the event of an accident involving an injury. Keep such records for a minimum of 5 years. It is a wise practice for all instructors to carry adequate personal liability insurance. Rates for such insurance have risen dramatically in recent years, but you should consider very seriously the consequences of being uninsured.

Step 1 Buoyancy

Different students, even in the same class, typically display a variety of buoyancy skill levels. You need a critical eye to observe their performance differences. The three criteria below—confidence, breath control, and body position—have been selected for you to use as either observation or evaluation tools. You may choose any one or all of these criteria, or you may select any of the items in the ''Keys to Success Checklist'' describing proper technique (listed in the participant's book, *Swimming: Steps to Success*). With practice, you can quickly develop a trained eye for differentiating three skill levels: beginning, novice, and accomplished.

Buoyancy Rating

CHECKPOINT	BEGINNING LEVEL	NOVICE LEVEL	ACCOMPLISHED LEVEL
Confidence	• Fearful • Tends to tilt head back • Fingers never release edge • 3- to 5-second submersion	• Uncertain • Hands ready to grab side • 5- to 8-second submersion	• Confident • Smooth submersion • Sinks a few inches and rises
Breath Control	• Must be reminded to breathe fully	• Breathes fully, short duration	• Holds for 15-20 seconds
Body Position	• Vertical • Hands at pool edge • Chin high	• Vertical • Hands 6 inches underwater	• Vertical • Hands at side

Error Detection and Correction for the Buoyancy Skill

As you observe several students, you will find that certain errors typically occur. Sometimes body language tells you more about the proficiency and mental state of a student than actual errors in technique. Look at the following list of errors and clues to attitude problems. If you observe any in your student, refer to the right-hand side of the page for suggestions on how to correct or alleviate it. Correct one error at a time.

ERROR 🚫	CORRECTION
1. Fingers remain on the pool edge.	1. Have student hold onto your fingers; lower him or her slowly into the water.
2. Student gets water in nose.	2. Have student hold chin lower and exhale one bubble through nose as nose goes underwater.
3. Student exhales while face is underwater.	3. Explain importance of full lungs to buoyancy.
4. Student closes eyes.	4. Tell student to watch wall to detect whether sinking.
5. Student sinks while reaching for the wall at end of float.	5. Tell student to raise hands very slowly and to hold breath until hands grasp side.
6. Student drifts away from wall.	6. Tell student not to arch back, but to keep chin down and to keep from pushing against the wall. The student shouldn't try floating in front of an inlet.

Selected Buoyancy Drills

1. Buoyancy Discovery Drill
[Corresponds to *Swimming*, Step 1, Drill 1]

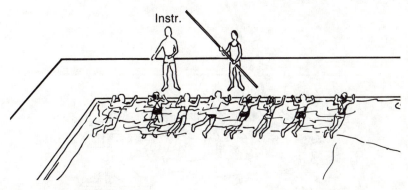

Group Management and Safety Tips

A demonstration of this drill, preferably in deep water, is important to reduce students' fears.

Place your students in shallow water (maximum depth of 5 feet) along the pool wall, with the tallest students toward the deeper end. The number of students that may be accommodated depends upon the size of the pool. Each student should have about 3 feet of wall space where the student's knees won't touch bottom.

Talk your students through the drill. Give individual help as required. Identify students who have marginal or negative buoyancy; fit them with float belts so they float with the waterline at eyebrow level.

Equipment

- Float belts of variable buoyancy for those few who need them.

Instructions to Class

- ''Hold the edge with two fingers.''
- ''Bend your knees to keep your feet off the bottom.''
- ''Take a big breath; hold it.''
- ''Look straight ahead.''
- ''Lower yourself very slowly, until there is no weight on your fingers. Stop.''
- ''Hold, then bring your fingers underwater.''

- ''See? You float!''
- ''Take hold of the pool edge, come up, and exhale.''

Student Option

- ''Continue to practice on your own, with your neighbor watching and correcting you.''

Student Keys to Success

- Slow, smooth execution
- Relaxed breath control

Student Success Goals

- Smooth, confident buoyancy float with
  (a) eyes closed
  (b) eyes open

To Reduce Difficulty

- Provide float belts, but gradually reduce buoyancy of belts.
- Increase confidence by giving individual aid.

To Increase Difficulty

- Have student keep eyes open.
- Increase breath-holding time.
- Have student raise hands out of water near shoulders and float with hands out and head submerged.

2. Deep-Water Buoyancy Discovery Drill

[Corresponds to *Swimming*, Step 1, Drill 2]

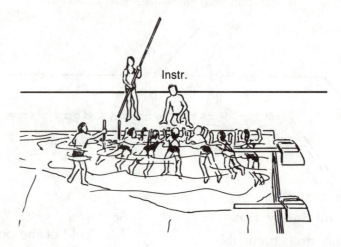

Instr.

Group Management and Safety Tips

Students enter deep water by ladder and go hand over hand along the edge to position. Lifeguard with reaching pole stands at the pool edge for safety and to give students confidence. Students try float one at a time, with instructor's full attention (about 1 minute each).

Equipment

- Variable buoyancy float belts for those who need them (probably one for each 15 students)
- Reaching poles (one or two)

Instructions to Class

- ''Do not start until I get to you.''
- ''Ready? Take a big breath. Lower yourself slowly, looking straight ahead, bring your fingers underwater and hold it. Okay, come on up.''

Student Options

- ''After I have watched you, practice the float WITHOUT RELEASING THE EDGE with a student partner watching.''
- ''With a student partner, practice extending your breath-holding time while holding the pool edge.''

Student Keys to Success

- Very slow, smooth immersion
- Bring hands confidently underwater
- Keep body straight, including knees, and remain vertical

Student Success Goal

- Without help from instructor, 5 repetitions of 15 seconds each with eyes open, knees and body straight, and hands under

To Reduce Difficulty

- Provide float belts.
- Allow floating with hands touching edge.
- Allow floating while holding your hand.
- Allow floating with fingers loosely circling a reaching pole held vertically in front of student.

To Increase Difficulty

- Assign longer breath-holding periods.
- Have student push self downward underwater to arm's length before releasing edge and floating to surface.
- Tell student to raise arms SLOWLY until fully extended directly overhead during float and, remaining vertical, to lower them SLOWLY to the sides again.

Step 2 Back Float

There are differences in persons' body structures that make back floats differ. Some people float horizontally with their toes out of water; others vary in position from horizontal to vertical. This variation is caused by bone structure and the ratios between fat tissue, muscle tissue, and lung capacity. In detecting errors in technique, you must separate factors due to body structure from those due to faulty technique.

Error Detection and Correction for the Back Float

Some typical errors in the back float made by beginning students are listed in *Swimming: Steps to Success*. In addition, look for the errors listed below. A possible correction for each error is listed on the right-hand side of the page.

ERROR

CORRECTION

1. Random foot or hand movements exist.

2. Hands come out of water while straight arms are moving beyond head, causing face to submerge.

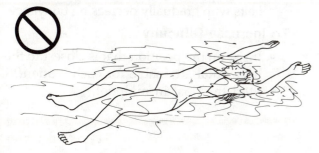

3. Even with full lungs, student still floats too low to allow breathing.

1. Impress on student that random movements are likely to cause face to submerge or to create waves that wash over face.

2. Have student raise arms more slowly, stopping frequently to allow feet to attain new balance point before continuing.

3. Provide float belt until student learns to scull.

Selected Back Float Drills

1. Beginning Back Float Drill
[Corresponds to *Swimming*, Step 2, Drill 2]

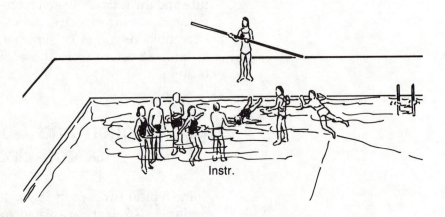

Instr.

Group Management and Safety Tips

Demonstrate the float technique.

It is very important for every student to have a pleasant, secure experience at this point. Spend one minute with each student and have the others watch. You must be in the water with your student to prevent submersion until the recovery is mastered. Stand *behind* the student and place one finger behind the neck for support and to build confidence as he or she tries this float.

Equipment

* Float belts perhaps necessary for one or two nonbuoyant students

Instructions to Class

* ''Put two fingers on the wall.''
* ''Straighten your elbows and arch your back.''
* ''Head back, ears under.''
* ''Big breath, hands under.''
* ''Hold it.''
* ''Quick breath.'
* ''Arms out and up slowly.''
* ''Quick breath, sit, scoop, stand.''

Student Option

* ''Pair off and practice with your buddy helping behind you.''

Student Keys to Success

* Easy, rhythmic breathing
* Smooth, full arm motions on recovery

Student Success Goal

* 5 consecutive floats—each held motionless for at least 30 seconds—and recoveries without help, without submerging, but with confidence

To Reduce Difficulty

* Allow apprehensive students to wear float belts with gradually decreasing buoyancy.

To Increase Difficulty

* Insist on the position that is closest to the horizontal attainable for each student.
* Start the float in midpool.

2. Deep-Water Back Float
[Corresponds to *Swimming*, Step 2, Drill 3]

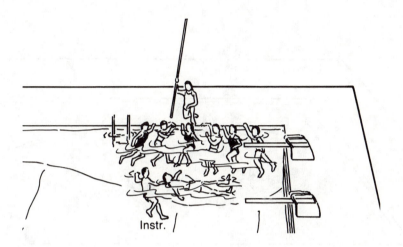

Instr.

Group Management and Safety Tips

Be sure your nonteaching lifeguard is at poolside with a reaching pole. Tell the students not to start until you get to them.

Stay at the head of the student as he or she does the float individually. Place a hand under the back of the neck to turn each student gently to guide him or her back to the wall.

Equipment

- Reaching pole for the lifeguard
- Float belts if necessary

Instructions to Class

- ''Do not start until I get to you.''
- ''Two fingers on the wall, head back, arms straight.''
- ''Big breath, float.''
- ''Breathe, arms out, hold still while I turn you around.''
- ''Grab the edge.''

Student Option

- None: ''Hold the edge and wait.''

Student Keys to Success

- Slow movement
- Quick, deep breaths
- Hold very still
- Float with confidence

Student Success Goal

- 3 repetitions in deep water, holding each float for at least 30 seconds, building confidence

To Reduce Difficulty

- Allow a float belt for the first float for those who are extremely fearful.

To Increase Difficulty

- Allow the confident students to pull gently with one arm to turn themselves in a circle back to the wall.

3. Back Float From Standing Position

[Corresponds to *Swimming*, Step 2, Drill 4]

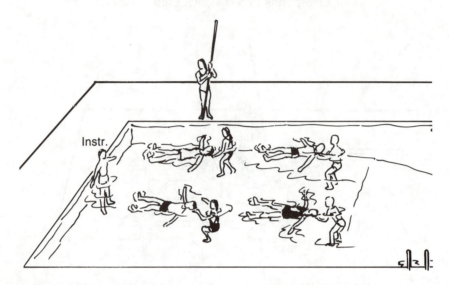

Instr.

Group Management and Safety Tips

Demonstrate the skill.

Allow students to work in pairs, with one standing at the head of the other to give confidence and prevent submersion. Students may be spread out in shallow area, preferably facing the same direction. You direct and give help where needed.

Holding perfectly still for 2-minute periods (or longer) can cause chilling. Interject some brisk warm-up activities (running, jumping, bobbing, bracket kicking) into this drill occasionally.

Equipment

- A large pace clock with sweep second hand at poolside to allow students to time themselves
- Float belts only for those of proven negative buoyancy

Instructions to Class

- "Work in pairs. Try to keep heels on the bottom as long as possible."
- "Stoop to chin depth, arms out, palms up, head back, ears under."
- "Drift back, hold, breathe, leave your feet on the bottom."
- "Sit, scoop, stand."

Student Option

- "Continue to practice, helping each other."

Student Keys to Success

- Easy, continuous motion
- Relax, breathe

Student Success Goal

- 3 consecutive confident, fluid-motion floats in shallow midpool for at least 2 minutes each.

To Reduce Difficulty

- Help from behind swimmer to keep the head from submerging from sudden movements or on recovery.

To Increase Difficulty

- Have your student experiment with the arm position to determine the exact position at which the heels begin to rise from the bottom.
- Have your student tighten the stomach muscles while floating until the body is perfectly straight, not arched, and try to bring the toes to the surface. A student may even have a small forward bend at the hips before achieving the toes-out position.

Step 3 Sculling

This beginner's use of sculling for forward propulsion is only the tip of the iceberg in sculling. It is an extremely versatile skill that can be performed in any position. Swimmers can scull with hands at hip level, at shoulder level, or overhead to propel themselves head-first, feetfirst, sideways, diagonally, or in circles, or even to pivot horizontally or vertically. It is often used unconsciously by swimmers to maintain position in the water. Furthermore, sculling is part of the breaststroke and crawl arm pulls.

It is very important that the beginning swimmer understands the concept of sculling and masters this first step in an extremely useful series of skills.

Error Detection and Correction in Sculling

Errors in sculling assume typical patterns. The student either gets the feel of sculling and uses it well, or it is completely useless and provides no propulsion at all. You will see a dramatic change as the student suddenly grasps the concept.

Look for the following errors in particular. If you find one of these errors, refer to the right-hand side of the page to find out how to correct it. Correct one error at a time.

ERROR

CORRECTION

1. Arm rotates from shoulder, making only fan-shaped semicircles with fingertips.

2. Student pushes water straight back along sides in finning motion.

3. Student needing support presses directly downward in a series of short thrusts.

4. Student fails to get the concept of rotating the arm from the shoulder at the end of each horizontal stroke.

1. Have student actually brush wall with relaxed wrists, emphasizing horizontal motion.

2. Insist that elbows be kept locked straight until concept is learned. Entire arm should be rotated from shoulder.

3. Place two small objects on a table. Have the student place a flat palm on each of the objects, wrists and elbows straight. Student should tilt hands to 45 degrees on inside of objects and push them apart, then rotate hands to outside of objects and push them together again. Have student keep pressing down on hands.

4. Standing, hold your arms out straight. Have the student, facing you, place palms against yours, arms straight. Tell student to press and follow your movements as you make the sculling motions.

Selected Sculling Drills

1. Variations on Sculling
[Corresponds to *Swimming*, Step 3, Drill 1]

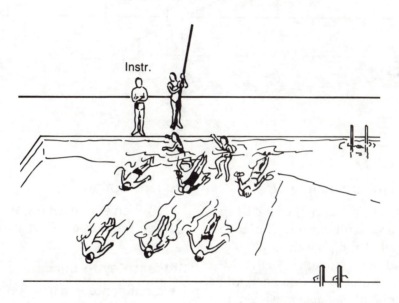

Instr.

Group Management and Safety Tips

Demonstrate sculling.

Have students try it on their own in shallow water for a few minutes. Watch to be sure no one sculls into deep water.

Have students line up along the side of the pool in shallow water and count off by threes (or fours). Then have all ''ones'' start sculling across the pool. When they have gone 15 feet, start the ''twos,'' an so on. This is called a *wave drill*.

Equipment

• A float belt or two, if necessary

Instructions to Class

• ''Line up against the wall.''
• ''Count off by threes.''
• ''On signal, start sculling across the pool. Make some wide and some narrow sculls.''
• ''Ones ready? Go!''

Student Option

• ''As soon as the last wave finishes, scull back on your own.''

Student Key to Success

• A smooth, relaxed figure eight

Student Success Goal

• Scull across pool, about 45 feet, with ease

To Reduce Difficulty

• Provide float belts for those who are non-buoyant.
• Shorten the desired sculling distance for those who have difficulty.

To Increase Difficulty

• Start the waves closer together, thus making the students go faster to keep ahead of the next wave.
• Make each wave a race.

2. Deep-Water Sculling
[Corresponds to *Swimming*, Step 3, Drill 2]

Instr.

Group Management and Safety Tips

Have students start at the corner of the deep end of the pool and scull close to the edge along the side wall of the pool in single file. You swim alongside each student until the student is in shallow water. Then go back and start the second student, swim alongside, and so on.

Have the lifeguard walking on the side with a reaching pole.

Equipment

- None

Instructions to Class

- ''Sit on the edge until I start you.''
- ''Scull all the way to the shallow end.''
- ''I'll stay beside you until you reach shallow water.''

Student Option

- ''When you reach the shallow end, practice sculling on your own until I get to you.''

Student Key to Success

- Confidence + relaxation = easy distance

Student Success Goal

- Scull 1 pool length, or 75 feet, in a slow, relaxed manner

To Reduce Difficulty

- Start student from a position in deep water, but only a few feet from the beginning of shallow water.
- Shorten the distance.

To Increase Difficulty

- Start each student from the center of the deep end, away from the sides (you stay nearby, alert).

3. Deep-Water Scull and Turn Drill

[Corresponds to *Swimming*, Step 3, Drill 4]

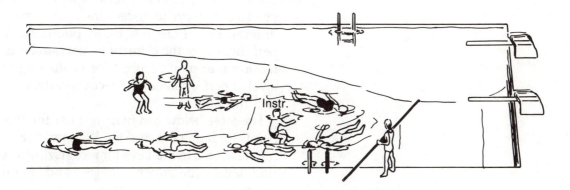

Group Management and Safety Tips

Demonstrate the skill.

Start the students in shallow water, but only a few feet from the beginning of deep water. Have them start about 15 feet from the side wall. They should turn toward the side wall so they are sculling toward safety as they turn. They need to scull only a few feet into the deep water before turning. Position yourself inside the turn, and have the students continue in a steady stream in single file, about 10 feet apart.

Equipment

- Possibly one or two float belts

Instructions to Class

- "In single file, about 10 feet apart, scull into the deep water, turn around me, and continue back into shallow water."

Student Option

- "When you reach shallow water, either scull out away from the wall and make a turn in the other direction or turn at the end wall to get back into line."

Student Keys to Success

- Steady propulsion
- Confidence and relaxation

Student Success Goal

- 5 deep-water turns in each direction

To Reduce Difficulty

- Provide float belts for nonbuoyant students.
- Lend your immediate presence for the apprehensive.

To Increase Difficulty

- Make the turn larger, requiring more time in deep water.
- Increase the distance by having students start farther toward the shallow end and swim farther toward the deep end before turning.

Step 4   Elementary Backstroke Arm Motion

Students vary in ability and experience. You need a critical eye to discern their performance differences. There are three points in the performance of the elementary backstroke arm motion that may be used for evaluating the level of performance: the recovery, the catch, and the pull.

The table below can help you use the three points for rating the student. With practice you can develop a trained eye for recognizing three skill levels; beginner, novice, and accomplished.

Elementary Backstroke Arm Motion Rating

CHECKPOINT	BEGINNING LEVEL	NOVICE LEVEL	ACCOMPLISHED LEVEL
Recovery	• Too fast • Hand tends to start catch before reaching top of shoulder • Thumbs away from sides	• Starts too soon • Slightly jerky • Thumbs touching sides	• Slow, easy, relaxed • Thumbs along sides • Fingertips to top of shoulder • Smooth
Catch	• Starts too early • Reach not high enough • Arm does not straighten • Too quick	• Starts from top • Reach is higher, but pull starts before arm stretched for catch • Arm not quite fully extended	• Starts from top • Reaches well above shoulder • Stretches to full extension • Fingertips catch before pull begins
Pull	• Short • Arm bent • No glide • Ineffective	• Arm not fully extended • Short glide • Not powerful	• Long, full powerful arm pull • Long, easy glide • Steamlined

Error Detection and Correction for the Elementary Back Arm Pull

Most of the typical errors made by beginners in the elementary backstroke arm motion are included in the evaluation chart on page 22 or in *Swimming: Steps to Success* . Look for the following errors in particular. If you find one of these errors, refer to the right-hand side of the page to find out how to correct it. Work on one error at a time.

ERROR    **CORRECTION**

1. Student has only a short, ineffective pull.	1. Tell the student not to think of moving the arms through the water, but to think instead of anchoring fingertips on something solid at extreme reach, slightly forward of the shoulder level, and pulling the body past fingertips.
2. There is no glide or glide is too short.	2. Have the student count out loud 4 one-second counts before starting recovery for next stroke.

Selected Elementary Backstroke Arm Motion Drills

1. *Shallow-Water Drill*
[Corresponds to *Swimming*, Step 4, Drill 1]

Instr.

Group Management and Safety Tips

Demonstrate the skill.

Have the students line up along the side of the pool in the shallow area, count off by threes (or fours), and go across the pool in waves. Allow at least 20 feet between waves. Have the students glide as far as they can on each stroke and count the strokes necessary to get to the other side. Be sure to ask each student how many strokes it took, or they will stop counting.

Repeat several times.

Equipment

- Possible float belts for the nonbuoyant

Instructions to Class

- ''Go when I call your number.''
- ''Glide as far as you can on each stroke.''
- ''Count how many strokes it took to get across. I'll be asking for the count.''
- ''Ones ready? Go!''

Student Option

- None

Student Keys to Success

- Full, solid, smooth arm pull
- Streamlined body: legs straight, toes pointed
- Glide until forward motion nearly stops
- Minimize negative forces during recovery

Student Success Goal

- 45 feet or more, averaging 5 feet per stroke (some variation allowed for the size and buoyancy of the student)

To Reduce Difficulty

- Allow less distance per stroke for smaller, weaker, and nonbuoyant students.

To Increase Difficulty

- Ask students to cut one or two strokes off the number required to cross the pool.

2. *Deep-Water Drill*
[Corresponds to *Swimming*, Step 4, Drill 2]

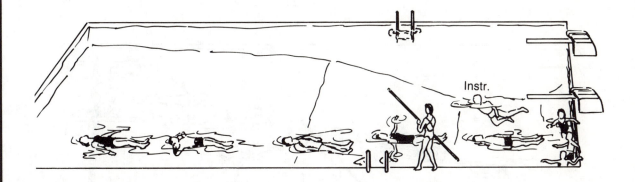

Group Management and Safety Tips

Have students begin at the deep end of the pool. They should go one at a time in single file and stay close to the side.

You should swim alongside until each reaches shallow water. The lifeguard should walk along the edge with a reaching pole.

Equipment

- None

Instructions to Class

- "Do not start until I come for you."
- "Full pulls. Swim to the shallow end wall."
- "Ready? Start."

Student Option

- "When you reach the shallow end, stay there and practice."

Student Keys to Success

- Exhale at end of glide and inhale on recovery
- Hold breath during glide

Student Success Goal

- 1 full pool length, or 75 feet, with smooth pulls and long glides

To Reduce Difficulty

- Reduce the distance and the stress by starting the student partway down the pool, closer to the shallow water.
- Float belts on the nonbuoyant are okay.

To Increase Difficulty

- Have the student swim from the deep corner to the diagonally opposite shallow corner. This requires longer distance and swimming farther from the edge.

3. Backstroke and Sculling Drill

[Corresponds to *Swimming*, Step 4, Drill 3]

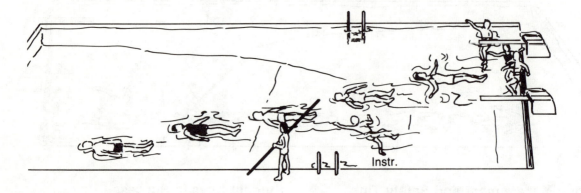

Group Management and Safety Tips

Demonstrate the drill.

Use a wave drill across the shallow end of the pool.

When students feel confident in the skills and the transition, line them up across the deep end of the pool and start them one at a time (stagger drill) for a full pool length. Let those who are least confident stay along the edge. Each student should change from sculling to stroking every 15-25 feet.

Stay in the water near each student at the start, and have the lifeguard on the edge with a reaching pole.

Equipment

• Possible float belts

Instructions to Class

• "Leave the wall on command" (applies to either wave or stagger drill).
• "Change from pull to scull frequently."
• "Go all the way to the shallow end."

Student Option

• "Continue to practice in the shallow end."

Student Keys to Success

• Smooth transition
• Easy breathing

Student Success Goal

• 4 or more transitions over a distance of one pool length (75 feet) or more

To Reduce Difficulty

• Keep the student in shallow water. Allow float belts for the nonbuoyant.

To Increase Difficulty

• Have the student continuously do a pull-glide-scull 5 feet, pull-glide-scull 5 feet, and so on.

4. Backstroke Pull and Turn Drill

[Corresponds to *Swimming*, Step 4, Drill 4]

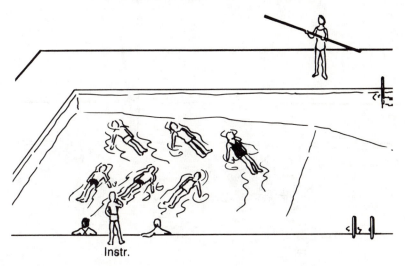

Instr.

Group Management and Safety Tips

Demonstrate the skill.

Use a wave drill in shallow water. Have the first wave start. On signal (whistle), they should pull only with their left arms, then only with their right arms at the second signal. Start the second wave at the third whistle, and the third wave three signals later, and so on. The result will be chaos, but it will be a lot of fun.

Be careful of the direction in which your swimmers are turning so none ends up in deep water inadvertently. Use a multiple-whistle ''all stop'' signal for safety.

Allow a short free time for students to practice turning on their own.

Equipment

- Float belts, if necessary

Instructions to Class

- ''Start with a backstroke pull when I call your number. At the first whistle pull only with the right arm. At the second whistle pull only with the left arm. Keep changing arms at each whistle.''
- ''Stop and stand immediately at three consecutive whistles.''

Student Option

- ''You can have a few minutes free practice time after the drill.''

Student Keys to Success

- Full arm pulls on turns
- Short glide on turns
- Keep body straight

Student Success Goal

- Multiple turns in each direction, smoothly and with a straight body

To Reduce Difficulty

- Let more time elapse between whistles.

To Increase Difficulty

- Intersperse sculling turns with pulling turns.
- Tell your students to decrease the number of pulls necessary to complete a 180-degree turn.

5. Deep-Water Backstroke Turn Drill
[Corresponds to *Swimming*, Step 4, Drill 5]

Group Management and Safety Tips

Demonstrate the skill.

Start students in single file at a depth of about 5 feet, and about 20 feet from deep water. Have them do the backstroke pull until they are in deep water. Then they should turn and swim back. Station yourself at the point where you want them to turn, so they do the turn around you. Have a student start from shallow water when the previous student is starting the turn.

Repeat the drill, having them turn in the opposite direction.

Equipment

- Float belts, if needed

Instructions to Class

- ''Start when the person ahead of you is in midturn.''
- ''Turn around me and swim back to the shallow end.''

Student Option

- ''At the shallow end, turn and complete the circle to your starting point.''

Student Keys to Success

- Full arm pulls
- Short glides during turns

Student Success Goal

- 5 deep-water turns in each direction with confidence

To Reduce Difficulty

- Allow more shallow water practice until swimmer is confident.

To Increase Difficulty

- Increase the distance prior to (and after) the turn.
- Make the deep-water turn a complete circle in addition to the regular 180 degrees.

Step 5 Support Kicking

It may be unnecessary to teach this skill to students who have considerable natural buoyancy. They may well progress directly to the next step, the crawl kick. However, support kicking aids anyone in leveling off from a vertical position a little faster than would occur from buoyancy alone.

Students enter a swimming class at various levels of competence and progress at varying rates. An experienced instructor is able to look at a skill performance, evaluate certain checkpoints within the performance, and classify the student as to competence level. In evaluating a student's support kicking, there are several aspects that an instructor can look for. Three of these are listed in the table below, along with guidelines to help in classifying the student in one of three skill levels.

Support Kick Rating

CHECKPOINT	BEGINNING LEVEL	NOVICE LEVEL	ACCOMPLISHED LEVEL
Body Position	• Sitting, hips bent • Chin down • Much splash from feet	• Horizontal • Tense • Knees break surface	• Horizontal • Relaxed • Few ripples result
Ankle-Foot Action	• Random: may be floppy or tense	• Fixed: may be pointed or hooked	• Working properly: foot hooked on upward stroke, pointed on downward stroke
Kick Direction	• Random: in and out, or up and down	• Usually up and down • Knees often break surface	• Circular ''bicycle'' action • Totally beneath the surface

Error Detection and Correction for the Support Kick

Some typical errors are listed in the participant's book, but understanding the purpose of the kick—pressing downward to give upward support—leads to error identification through common sense: All downward motions must be maximized, upward motions minimized, and extraneous motions eliminated. Look for the following errors in particular. If you find one of these errors, refer to the right-hand side of the page to find out how to correct it.

ERROR

CORRECTION

1. Feet kick in and out horizontally like pistons.

1. Assign land drill or shallow-water bracket drill. Guide student's legs through proper motions.

2. There is no downward thrust of feet.

2. In shallow water, hold student's shoulders just out of the water so feet sink and student must extend toes to touch rungs of ladder in side of pool. Have student extend toes onto ladder and press down to walk feet up ladder.

3. Knees and feet break surface.

3. Call student's attention to the fault. Have him or her slow the kick down and place legs and feet more carefully.

Selected Support Kick Drills

1. *Support Kick Bracket Drill*
[Corresponds to *Swimming*, Step 5, Drill 1]

Instr.

Group Management and Safety Tips

Demonstrate the skill.

Students may be lined up along the edge of the pool in shallow water, their backs to the wall and their elbows hooked on the edge behind them. Keeping their heads and shoulders out of the water ensures that their feet will sink and that a support kick will be needed to raise the feet to the surface.

On command, they should ''pedal a bike,'' pressing down with the soles of their feet to make their feet rise.

Equipment

- None

Instructions to Class

- ''Back against the wall, elbows hooked on the edge.''
- ''On command, step up to the top of the water by using a bicycle kick.''
- ''Ready? Kick!''

Student Option

- ''If it seems easier, hold onto the edge with your hands over your shoulders.''

Student Keys to Success

- Step to top smoothly
- No splash at all

Student Success Goal

- Step to the surface 5 times and maintain feet at the surface, kicking, for 1 minute

To Reduce Difficulty

- Stand in the water facing the student who needs help. Hold your hands out so the student's toes just brush your palms during the kick. Have the student concentrate on pressing against your hands to raise his or her feet.
- Allow the student to slide down farther in the water so the head and shoulders are virtually floating.

To Increase Difficulty

- Have the student wear a weight belt of about 5 pounds around the hips.

2. Shallow-Water Support Kick and Pull Drill

[Corresponds to *Swimming*, Step 5, Drill 4]

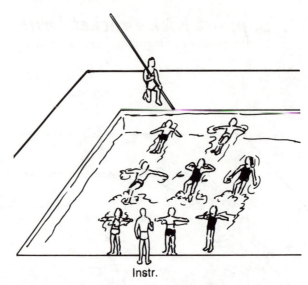

Instr.

Group Management and Safety Tips

Use a wave drill going across the pool in shallow water. Have the first wave take a back float position with heels on the bottom and arms straight out to the sides. They should then use the support kick to get their feet to the surface. They should begin stroking, continue to kick about 15 feet, then stop stroking, remaining in a motionless float until the feet sink. They repeat this sequence until reaching the other side of the pool.

Have the second wave start when the first wave starts the kick for the second time.

Equipment

- Float belts for the nonbuoyant

Instructions to Class

- ''Start when I call your number. Kick to the surface and pull two strokes. Stop, let your feet sink, and do it again.''
- ''Ones ready? Go!''

Student Option

- None

Student Keys to Success

- Keep hips up, do not sit, when starting kick
- Begin stroking smoothly when feet reach surface

Student Success Goal

- Level-off from feet-down position 5 times with confidence

To Reduce Difficulty

- Stand in the water facing the student, who is floating with feet down. Allow student to walk his feet up your body until the concept is understood.

To Increase Difficulty

- Have nonbuoyant students try the drill without float belts or with reduced flotation.

3. *Level-Off in Deep Water With Support Kick*
[New drill]

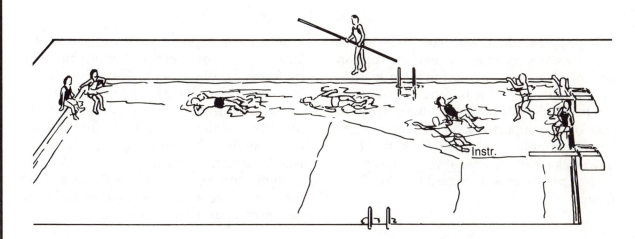

Group Management and Safety Tips

Demonstrate the skill.

The vertical position in deep water is the most likely position to cause panic in beginners. For this reason the level-off process is extremely important. It must be monitored carefully to ensure that all students achieve success, and none are unduly frightened.

Have the students attempt this skill close to the edge of the pool. Take each student individually until you are sure the student is confident. Then have the student proceed down the length of the pool under the watchful eye of a lifeguard with a reaching pole, leveling off repeatedly. Stay in the water beside the student until the skill is mastered.

Have the very buoyant student, who would normally float horizontally, start in a vertical position.

Equipment

- Float belts for the nonbuoyant (do not have student swim in deep water without belt until you are sure of his or her ability to maintain support)

Instructions to Class

- "Do not start until I call for you."
- "Start in a vertical position, holding the side of the pool."
- "Step your feet up to the surface and pull."
- "Continue to the shallow end but allow your feet to drop several times, and kick them back up again."

Student Option

- "Try the drill several times more in shallow water, using sculling as well as pulling."

Student Keys to Success

- Slow, calm, confident footsteps to the surface
- Easy, constant forward propulsion

Student Success Goal

- 5 or more deep-water level-offs with increasing confidence

To Reduce Difficulty

- Remain in the water at the student's side. Keep one hand in contact with the student's back for confidence.

To Increase Difficulty

- Stay farther away from the student.
- Start student farther from the edge.
- Have the swimmer level off, go to vertical, then level off again without sculling or stroking, keeping arms at sides.

Step 6   Back Crawl Kicking

Nonbuoyant students who have just set aside float belts as a result of learning the support kick may well have to resort to them again in learning this kick. The upward thrust of the foot here is directly opposite to the downward push of the support kick. In the long run, the forward propulsion gained from the back crawl kick offsets any negative buoyancy and allows the students to discard the float belts again.

Swimmers display a variety of skill levels. Develop a critical eye for observing their performance differences. Three back crawl kick checkpoints have been selected that you may use as observation and evaluation tools. You may use the checkpoints below and any items in the ''Keys to Success Checklist'' (see *Swimming: Steps to Success*, Step 6) for recognizing proper technique. With practice you can differentiate three skill levels: beginner, novice, and accomplished.

Back Crawl Kick Rating

CHECKPOINTS	BEGINNING LEVEL	NOVICE LEVEL	ACCOMPLISHED LEVEL
Foot-Ankle Motion	• Rigidly hooked or pointed	• Pointed, rigidity varying	• Completely floppy: pointed on upward thrust, hooked on downward thrust • Slight toe turn-in
Knee-Leg Motion	• In-out piston motion or bicycling • Feet and knees splashing • Sitting up at hips	• Up-down motion, but knees break surface • Foot stays deep • Hips down	• Up-down motion coming from hips, with foot whipping just below surface • Raising mound of water, but making no splash • Hips up
Propulsion	• Very little	• Some, but with splash	• Smooth, easy, fast

Error Detection and Correction for the Back Crawl Kick

Swimming: Steps to Success lists several common errors in the back crawl kick. Some of them are a result of learning the support kick just prior to the propulsion kick; students still persist in pressing downward. The concept of the back crawl kick, though, centers on an upward and backward thrust of the foot. One additional error deserves mention. If you find it, refer to the right-hand column for a suggestion on how to correct it.

ERROR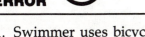

CORRECTION

1. Swimmer uses bicycling, circular motion, or piston action of the legs.

1. Assign bracket drill on edge of pool. Hold a beach ball directly over student's toes. Have student practice kicking it with the top of the toes.

Selected Back Crawl Drills

1. Shallow-Water Kickboard Drill for Back Crawl Kick
[Corresponds to *Swimming*, Step 6, Drill 3]

Instr.

Group Management and Safety Tips

Demonstrate the skill.

This drill is best accomplished as a stagger or wave drill. Line the students up along the side of the pool to go across the shallow end. Start each student, or each wave of students, when the previous student or wave is about 15 feet out.

Be sure the kickboard is held tightly to the chest to preclude any "sitting" position of the hips. Emphasize that the hips be held high and the kick remains totally beneath, or behind, the swimmer. Tell the student to imagine that he or she is digging the toes into the mud and pushing backward with the top of the toes.

Equipment

- May need float belts, but discourage their use or reduce the flotation

Instructions to Class

- "Start when I call your number."
- "Hold the board close to your chest."
- "Kick all the way across."
- "Ones ready? Go!"

Student Option

- None

Student Keys to Success

- Ankle is perfectly relaxed and floppy
- Toes flip upward at end of kick, but do not break the surface
- A mound of water, but little or no splash, appears at the toes

Student Success Goal

- 5 full pool widths

To Reduce Difficulty

- Allow float belts if necessary.
- Reduce the desired distance so student can achieve success.
- Give individual help and encouragement.

To Increase Difficulty

- Do the same drill without the kickboard, hands at sides.

2. Deep-Water Kickboard Drill for Back Crawl

[Corresponds to *Swimming*, Step 6, Drill 4]

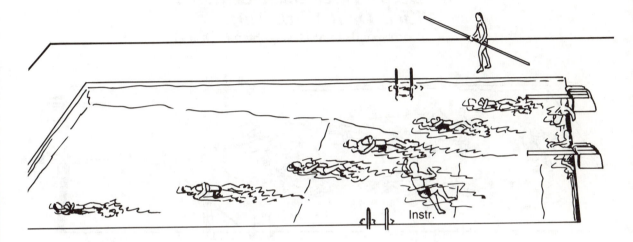

Group Management and Safety Tips

The safest method for running this drill would be single file along the edge of the pool. However, your students are now holding a kickboard, which contributes to their safety. If there are students who are confident, you may run this as a stagger drill, beginning with the students lined up across the deep end of the pool. Thus, some would be going down the middle of the pool.

Stay in the water with them until they reach the shallow water and be sure the lifeguard is on the edge with a reaching pole.

Equipment

- Kickboards

Instructions to Class

- ''Start on command and kick the full length of the pool.''
- ''Ready? Go!''

Student Option

- ''When you reach the shallow end, try kicking across the pool without the kickboard.''

Student Key to Success

- Easy, nontiring, relaxed kick

Student Success Goal

- Kick nonstop the full length of the pool, or 75 feet

To Reduce Difficulty

- Shorten the distance expected.
- Reduce your student's fear by allowing him or her to go along the pool edge and by your staying alongside.

To Increase Difficulty

- Have your student go diagonally from deep corner to shallow corner.
- Have the swimmer remove float belt.
- Have the student kick from the shallow to the deep end.

3. Deep-Water Back Crawl Kick Drill With Turn
[Corresponds to *Swimming*, Step 6, Drill 7]

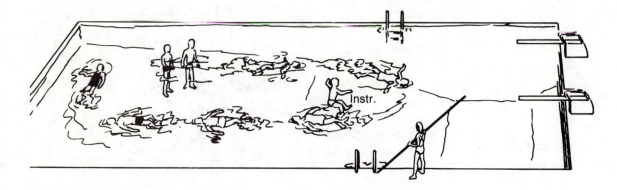

Group Management and Safety Tips

Line up students in single file in shallow water, facing the deep end of the pool. Have students kick and pull out into deep water, do the turn around you, and continue back into shallow water. Position yourself so the turn will be toward the edge where the lifeguard stands with reaching pole. Start them far enough apart that you can watch each one through the turn.

Don't forget to have them practice turning both ways.

Equipment

- Float belts if necessary

Instruction to Class

- ''Do not start until I call for you.''
- ''Kick and pull, do a turn around me, and continue to the shallow end.''

Student Option

- ''When you reach the shallow end, turn and complete the circle to the starting point in order to go again.''

Student Key to Success

- Easy, confident, relaxed swimming

Student Success Goal

- 5 turns in each direction, with rests between

To Reduce Difficulty

- Give close personal supervision to foster confidence.

To Increase Difficulty

- Make the turn a large, wide turn that takes in the entire width of the pool.
- Require a complete circle of the circumference of the pool.
- Require sharp, right-angle turns.

Step 7 Prone Float

There are several possible approaches to teaching the prone float. One of the most common methods involves simply having the student push off from the pool bottom or facedown from the side. Here we have chosen to relate the prone float to the buoyancy skills the student has already learned. Floating is a known skill. Now we will concentrate on a simple variation in balance that alters the body position of the student to produce a prone float:

Remaining motionless with the back arched and lungs filled with air *always* produces a back float, but remaining motionless with the hips bent forward *always* results in a prone float.

This is a very simple skill. Perhaps its most difficult aspect for some is deliberately putting the face underwater. You may find that the recovery to standing position is more difficult in the prone float than in the back float, particularly for students with very buoyant legs.

Error Detection and Correction for the Prone Float

There are very few errors the student can make in a skill so simple. However, if you find any of the following typical errors, look to the right-hand side of the page for a suggested correction.

ERROR

CORRECTION

ERROR	CORRECTION
1. Student has tendency to roll over.	1. This is caused by arching the back. The body cannot roll if it is bent slightly forward. Spreading the legs and arms apart also prevents rolling.
2. Student has difficulty in regaining standing position.	2. This is caused by student reaching for bottom while still in semihorizontal position. Stress that the student tuck first—then press—and wait until fully vertical before attempting to stand.
3. Feet remain on bottom.	3. Nonbuoyant student needs to wear a float belt. Have him or her shift position of belt slightly lower on chest for this float.

Selected Prone Float Drills

1. *Jellyfish Float*
[New drill]

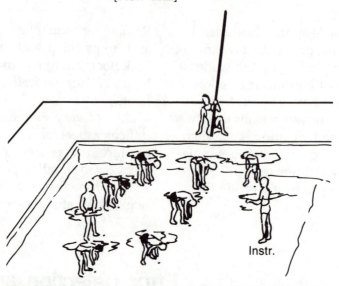

Instr.

Group Management and Safety Tips

Demonstrate the skill.

Give each student a diving ring or some other small object that sinks (a nickel, for instance). Have the students stand in water that is just a little more than waist-deep, place the object on the bottom, and keep one foot in contact with it.

Now tell them the object of the drill is to pick up the object SLOWLY. Have them take a deep breath, hold it, put their faces into the water, and SLOWLY slide their hands down their legs until they reach the object. Let them discover that it is impossible to reach the object because they will float. For a safe recovery they must slide the hands back up again or they will have a hard time getting their feet down. Stay alert for the student who has trouble regaining a standing position.

Equipment

- A diving ring or small sinking object for each student. (Give them each a nickel and tell them they can keep it if they can reach it *following the rules*. You will lose nickels only to the nonbuoyant students and those in water too shallow.)

Instructions to Class

- ''Put one toe on this object.''
- ''Put your hands on your thighs.''
- ''Take a deep breath.''
- ''Slide your hands down slowly to your feet to pick up the object.''
- ''If you can't reach the object, slide your hands back up your legs to stand.''

Student Option

- ''Continue to try to pick up the object, but slowly and with an even deeper breath.''

Student Key to Success

- Smooth, slow movements

Student Success Goal

- Discovery that the body floats in a jellyfish position

To Reduce Difficulty

- Remain in contact with those who are frightened.
- Reduce the difficulty of *reaching the object* by allowing them to ''jump'' down.

To Increase Difficulty

- Move to deeper water.
- Lengthen the breath-holding time.

2. Jellyfish Prone Float
[Corresponds to *Swimming*, Step 7, Drill 1]

Instr.

Group Management and Safety Tips

Demonstrate the skill.

Have the students stand in chest-deep water. Make sure they have space to stretch out without kicking each other. Have the students take a big breath (and with float belts for the nonbuoyant), do a jellyfish float, then straighten the body out into a prone float. They should hold the prone float for as long as is comfortable and return to the jellyfish position before attempting to stand. Be alert to those who hurry to stand. They will not first return to the jellyfish position and may have difficulty getting to their feet.

Equipment

* Float belts for the nonbuoyant students

Instructions to Class

* ''Slide your hands down your legs until you float.''
* ''Stretch out into a prone float and hold it.''
* ''Press strongly with your hands as you bring them back to your knees.''
* ''Slide your hands back up your legs to stand.''

Student Option

* ''Try again but tuck your knees as you press your arms to stand.''

Student Key to Success

* All movements smooth and confident

Student Success Goal

* Hold each prone position for more than 10 seconds

To Reduce Difficulty

* Shorten the expected breath-holding time.
* Aid swimmer in regaining feet until skill has been mastered.

To Increase Difficulty

* Increase the breath-holding time.

3. *Prone Float With Kickboard From Wall*
[Corresponds to *Swimming*, Step 7, Drill 3]

Instr.

Group Management and Safety Tips

Line up students with backs to the side wall in the shallow end. Have them count off into groups for wave drill. Instruct the students to push off the wall as hard as they can into a prone float. They should streamline their bodies, hold their breath, and glide for distance. Warn them that they must press down on their kickboards to stand, and to lift on the boards to keep their feet up.

Have each wave stand firm where they stop to make a target goal for the next wave to surpass. They will cheat, so have some fun with it.

Equipment

- Kickboards and float belts

Instructions to Class

- ''Start when I call your number.''
- ''Push off the wall hard, and glide as far as you can.''
- ''Stand at that spot to see whether anyone can beat you.''

Student Option

- ''Push off again from the bottom and glide to the other side.''

Student Keys to Success

- Complete body streamlining
- Breath-holding ability

Student Success Goal

- Any distance greater than 15 feet

To Reduce Difficulty

- Make the goal a time goal instead of a distance goal (e.g., ''How long can you hold your breath?'' or ''Can you hold longer than your neighbor?'').
- Stand in front of the student to create a visible goal.

To Increase Difficulty

- Have students continue to push off the bottom and float until they reach the other side of the pool.
- Repeat the drill without kickboards.

4. Prone Float From Wall
[Corresponds to *Swimming*, Step 7, Drill 5]

Group Management and Safety Tips

Arrange and conduct the drill as in the previous drill but be in the water ready to assist those who may have trouble getting back to their feet. Diving from the edge to assist such students embarrasses them and calls attention to their ineptness. Help is much less dramatic if you are already in the water.

Equipment

- Float belt for the nonbuoyant student (cuts glide length)

Instructions to Class

- ''When I call your number, push off with arms streamlined.''
- ''Glide as far as you can.''
- ''Stand at that point and wait to see whether anyone can beat you.''
- ''Tuck your knees and press hard with your hands to get your feet back down.''

Student Option

- ''Push off from the bottom and continue to glide across the pool.''

Student Keys to Success

- Full, smooth push-off
- Body fully streamlined, stretched

Student Success Goal

- A glide of 20 feet or more

To Reduce Difficulty

- Reduce the distance goal.
- Change the goal to a time goal.
- Assist those who need help in standing.

To Increase Difficulty

- Have students drop underwater for the push off and float to the surface during the glide. Some students should be able to glide all the way across the pool (45 feet).

Step 8   Beginner Kick

The beginner kick is the first attempt at propulsion in the prone position. Some support and propulsion can be derived from pressing in a downward and backward direction alternately with each foot and lower leg.

The beginner kick is a crude skill at best; that's how it got its name. It would be difficult to evaluate its performance for the purpose of classifying a student's level as beginner, novice, or accomplished. Perhaps it should be evaluated on the grounds of whether the propulsion and support it provides is poor, fair, or good. It is a transition skill that leads to the crawl kick, or flutter kick, which *can* be evaluated as beginner, novice, or accomplished.

Error Detection and Correction for the Beginner Kick

Even in the beginner kick's crude form, there are correct and incorrect ways to perform it. Look for the following errors in particular. If you find one of these errors, refer to the right-hand side of the page to find out how to correct it.

ERROR

CORRECTION

1. Legs have in-out, piston action similar to crawling.

1. Have student hold edge of pool with both hands as you manipulate his or her legs in proper motion. Stress not bringing knee under body, but kicking only lower leg and foot with hips straight.

2. Feet kick totally out of water.

2. Have student lift chin to look forward underwater, rather than looking down at bottom. Be sure hips are not bent.

3. Swimmer actually moves backward (toward feet) while floating and kicking hard.

3. This error is not uncommon, but most instructors are surprised to see it. It is the result of kicking downward with ankles fully hooked or hooking feet while they are moving downward. Have the student point toes on the downward thrust, if the ankle is flexible. If the ankle is too inflexible (in older adults, especially), have the student emphasize the backward thrust rather than the downward thrust.

Selected Beginner Kick Drills

1. Beginner Kick and Breathing With Kickboard
[Corresponds to *Swimming*, Step 8, Drill 3]

Instr.

Group Management and Safety Tips

Demonstrate the skill, with particular emphasis on the breathing.

At this stage, the students will have formed a habit of stopping whenever they need a breath. This drill should emphasize the need for continuing to kick while breathing.

Use a wave drill from the side of the pool in the shallow end. Teach the students to exhale slowly into the water. They should press on the kickboards just hard enough to get their chins up to the surface, grab a breath, and drop their chins to exhale. As soon as you can determine who they are, start the fastest students in the first wave.

Equipment

- Kickboards (no float belts should be needed)

Instructions to Class

- "When I call your number, hold the kickboard at arm's length and kick across the pool."

- "Tilt your head back to get your chin to water level and grab a breath."
- "Put your face down into the water to exhale."

Student Option

- "If you wish, keep your head up as you kick and exhale. However, it is easier to exhale into the water."

Student Key to Success

- Press on board only when breathing

Student Success Goal

- Continuous kicking and breathing across the pool, or for 45 feet

To Reduce Difficulty

- Shorten the distance expected.
- Allow student to pull kickboard back under chin and to keep head up.

To Increase Difficulty

- Have your students try the same drill without the kickboard, pressing their hands on the water to rise and breathe.
- Time the distance or race for speed.

2. *Beginner Kick Level-Off*
[New drill]

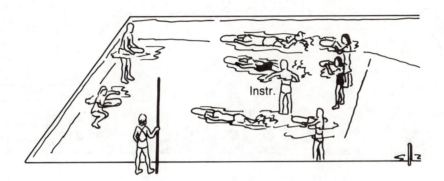

Group Management and Safety Tips

Demonstrate the skill.

Have students line up across the pool in shoulder-deep water facing the shallow end, with kickboards. Use a wave drill. On command, each wave starts by putting faces in the water and, without a push-off, starting to kick to bring their feet to the surface (leveling off) as quickly as possible. As soon as their feet have reached the surface, they are to stop and start over at that point.

Start a new wave when the previous wave has progressed toward the shallow end about 15 feet.

Repeat the drill with no kickboards.

Equipment

- Kickboards

Instructions to Class

- ''When I call your number, put your face in the water and start kicking your feet up behind you. Lift on the board with your hands to make your feet come up quicker.''
- ''When you need a breath, stop, get a breath, and level off again. Continue to the shallow end.''

Student Option

- ''Try to get your feet up by stepping back and pressing with your toes on the water, rather than by kicking. In other words, pedal a bike backward.''

Student Keys to Success

- Smooth kick, not frantic
- No jump at the start

Student Success Goal

- Confidence in leveling off from a vertical position, regardless of distance

To Reduce Difficulty

- Start swimmer in shallower water.
- Stay within touching distance to help student's confidence.

To Increase Difficulty

- Have the student start by sinking underwater and pushing off the bottom (without a board).

3. *Deep-Water Level-Off*
[New drill]

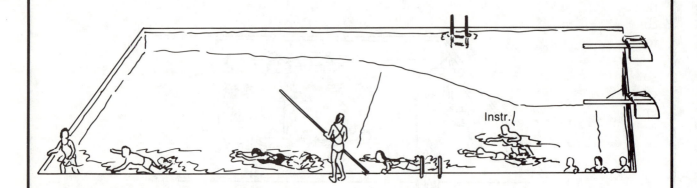

Group Management and Safety Tips

Demonstrate the skill.

Have the class start in single file in the corner of the deep end of the pool, without kickboards. Each student in turn should hang onto the side of the pool with one hand, facing the shallow end. Beginning in a vertical position, the student should release the wall on command, place his or her face in the water, and kick to a horizontal position facing the shallow end. When a new breath is needed, the student should grasp the wall with the nearest hand, come to a vertical position, and repeat the exercise.

You must be in the water, watching each student, especially when he or she reaches for the wall to get a new breath. Have the lifeguard walking along the edge with a reaching pole. Be watchful that the student does not inadvertently turn away from the wall while kicking. You must be sure that this is a good experience for the student, not a frightening one.

Equipment

- Float belts for the nonbuoyant

Instructions to Class

- "Do not start until I am with you."
- "Hold the side with one hand. Move away from the deep end far enough that you will not kick the wall behind you."
- "When you need a breath, grab the wall, get a breath, and start over."
- "Keep going to the shallow end."

Student Option

- "Step way up behind you with each foot in turn. Try to get your feet to the surface in 2 steps."

Student Key to Success

- Calmly step up behind and press down with the foot

Student Success Goal

- 5 or more consecutive successful level-offs

To Reduce Difficulty

- Have the lifeguard trail the end of the reaching pole between the arms of the student, so the student has the knowledge that it can be grabbed at any time.

To Increase Difficulty

- Have the student release the wall and sink under before starting to kick to the surface and level off.

Step 9 Beginner Pull

The beginner pull is really the underwater portion of the crawl stroke pull; it is a relatively complicated procedure starting in very crude form and progressing to perfection.

Students display a variety of skill levels; some progress faster than others. Develop a critical eye for observing performance differences. Three checkpoints have been selected that you may use as observation and evaluation tools. Use these checkpoints below or the items in the "Keys to Success Checklist" (see *Swimming: Steps to Success*, Step 9) to recognize proper technique. With practice, you can quickly develop a trained eye for differentiating three skill levels: beginner, novice, and accomplished.

Beginner Pull Rating

CHECKPOINT	BEGINNING LEVEL	NOVICE LEVEL	ACCOMPLISHED LEVEL
Pull	• Elbow low • "Dog paddle" • Elbow leads • Pull stops at waist	• Elbow straight • Presses down • Pulls deep • Pull stops at waist	• Elbow high • Hand digs in • 90-degree arm bend • Pulls in center line • Pulls to thigh
Recovery	• Starts at waist • Too deep • Reaches only to head	• Starts at waist • Pushes water with hand • No stretch • No glide	• Hand and elbow in • Minimum resistance • "Sneaks" hand back • Stretches ahead • Glides
Coordination	• Arms always opposite • Both arms working simultaneously • Short, fast movements	• Arms nearly opposite • Both arms working simultaneously • Slower, longer movements	• Arms overlap: one arm glides while other arm pulls • One arm pulling at a time • Slower, longer strokes

Error Detection and Correction for the Beginner Pull

As you observe your students, you will find certain errors typically occurring. Look for the following problems in particular. If you find one of these errors, refer to the right-hand side of the page to find out how to correct it. Correct only one error at a time.

ERROR

CORRECTION

1. Student uses short, "piston" pulls: typical "dog paddle."

2. Arm presses down.

3. One arm pulls while the other recovers.

1. Have student start from stretched float and pull from stretched position until thumb touches thigh.

2. Tell swimmer to raise elbow at start, pull with elbow bent at 90 degrees. Stress pulling straight back just under chest.

3. Stress "touch and go": Forward hand goes only when other hand touches it. Stress floating and pulling with one arm at a time, gliding on one arm while the other pulls.

Selected Beginner Pull Drills

1. Beginner Pull With Mask, Snorkel

[Corresponds to *Swimming*, Step 9, Drill 4]

Instr.

Group Management and Safety Tips

Demonstrate the skills.

If only a few masks and snorkels are available, have the rest of the class practice on the previous drills (1, 2, and 3 in *Swimming: Steps to Success*) while you fit masks and teach snorkel use to those for whom equipment is available. Then switch off. If masks are unavailable or do not fit, snorkels alone may be used, but a headband of some sort must be used to hold the snorkel upright.

Your students must be taught to "clear" the snorkels by puffing. Some students may have difficulty, breathing water when using a snorkel without a mask; have them use nose clips. It will take some time for your students to get used to the snorkels, but the results are worth it.

Equipment

- Masks or headbands
- Snorkels
- A few noseclips
- Leg floats, possibly

Instructions to Class

- "Keep your head down, breathe through the snorkel, pull across the pool."
- "Number ones ready? Go!"

Student Option

- "Those who must wait for a mask and snorkel, practice by holding your breath and pulling until equipment becomes available."

Student Keys to Success

- Float easily
- Breathe in normal rhythm
- Pull gently and fully

Student Success Goal

- Easy, relaxed pulling across the pool, or 45 feet

To Reduce Difficulty

- Take time to teach mask and snorkel use.
- Allow practice of floating and breathing with masks and snorkels *without* pulling or kicking.

To Increase Difficulty

- Have swimmer use snorkels *without* masks *or* noseclips.
- Make student deliberately pull head underwater so snorkel clearing will be necessary.

2. *Turning With Beginner Pulls, Mask, Snorkel, Leg Float*

[Corresponds to *Swimming*, Step 9, Drill 5]

Group Management and Safety Tips

Demonstrate the drill yourself (or have it demonstrated), so the students know exactly what is expected.

Have your students line up along the side of the pool in the shallow area. Because this wave drill requires left and right turns, your students need plenty of room. Only three should be in each wave. Divide the total number of students by three, using the result as the "count-off" number. This results in having groups of three. (Example: 18 in the class. Divide 18 by 3. Result equals 6. Count off by 6. A wave drill would thus have 6 waves of 3 students.)

Warn the students to stay in shallow water (with masks, they are easily able to see where deep water starts). Watch them very closely to assure that they do so. Have the lifeguard watching on the opposite side of the pool. Prearrange that the whistle will be an "all-stop" signal (everyone stops immediately where they are).

Each student in a wave has a mask, snorkel, and leg float. On command, they should begin to pull across the pool. After 3 strokes, students turn their heads and reach to the left while stroking to make a left turn of about 45 degrees. They then turn to the right 90 degrees and continue to make 90-degree turns in alternate directions until they reach the opposite pool wall.

Start the next wave only when the preceding wave is 2/3 across the pool.

Equipment

- Masks and snorkels
- Leg floats
- Whistle

Instructions to Class

- "Start when your number is called."
- "Continue to turn left and right across the pool."
- "Stop immediately at the whistle."

Student Option

- "Upon reaching the other side, stay close to the wall but practice floating motionless, using the leg floats and breathing through the snorkel. Be ready to come back the same way when your number is called."

Student Key to Success

- Relaxed, unhurried turns in each direction

Student Success Goal

- At least 4 turns in each direction

To Reduce Difficulty

- Have your student swim to midpool, turn 180 degrees, and return to side.
- Start a wave when the preceding one has started back. If the second wave waits until the first wave is coming back, the second-wave students can see where to swim to avoid collisions.

To Increase Difficulty

- Have each wave turn and start back immediately upon reaching the other side, thus having to use turns to avoid colliding with the oncoming waves of students.

3. Deep-Water Turns, Beginner Pull, Mask, Snorkel, Floats

[Corresponds to *Swimming*, Step 9, Drill 7]

Group Management and Safety Tips

Your students need leg floats, masks, and snorkels. Have your class line up in single file from the center of the shallow end of the pool to the 5-foot depth mark, facing the deep end. Station yourself about 15 feet into the deep water so that each student in turn can pull out past you, turn around you, and pull back into the shallow water. Insist on a rather wide turn (10-foot radius). Start the students far enough apart so only two are in deep water at one time. Have the lifeguard on the side of the deep-water area with a reaching pole, so student returns between you and the lifeguard.

Equipment

- Masks and snorkels
- Leg floats

Instructions to Class

- "Do not start until I call for you."
- "Pull out to me, make a wide turn to the right around me, and pull back into shallow water."
- "On the second trip, turn to the left around me."
- "Breathe through your snorkel all the way."

Student Option

- "When you get back to shallow water, continue to pull to the shallow end, make a turn, and return to the starting point. Wait there until I call you again."

Student Keys to Success

- Easy, relaxed, full pulls
- Normal breathing rate

Student Success Goal

- 2 turns in each direction, with rest when needed

To Reduce Difficulty

- Swim right beside your student until the turn is complete. Then have the lifeguard trail the reaching pole directly in front of the student's mask until he or she is back in shallow water.

To Increase Difficulty

- Have the student turn a full circle around you in addition to the regular 180-degree turn.

Step 10 Breathing

This skill does not lend itself well to performance classification into beginner, novice, and accomplished levels. It should be evaluated on the basis of ease of accomplishment and of time elapsed or distance swum between swallows of water (and there will be swallows!).

Error Detection and Correction in Rhythmic Breathing

Detecting errors in breathing is easy: Just look for the coughing student! Correcting breathing problems is hard, though, for it takes students much practice over a long period of time to develop good breathing habits. There are technique faults, however, that the instructor must try to remedy; otherwise, the student may never develop the correct technique. Look for the following problems in particular. If you find them, refer to the right-hand side of the page to find out how to correct them. Work on one error at a time, unless two or more seem interrelated.

ERROR 🚫

CORRECTION

1. Swimmer is breathless.

1. This is usually caused by instinctively retaining too much air during exhalation. Explain that no new air can be taken in until there is room for it. Therefore, the student must exhale more fully to make room. "Humming" the air out makes it easier.

2. Head is raised too high.

2. Only constant effort on the part of the student over a period of time can correct this. However, the head cannot be raised too high without the arms exerting downward pressure on the water. If the swimmer can eliminate this downward pressure by technique corrections, the head is forced to stay lower. Try to drill swimmer without supports such as kickboards as soon as possible. Then correct the stroke so pressure is all backward, not downward. Drill on breathing in an unsupported, motionless floating position.

3. Student inhales water.

3. If student is side-breathing, encourage rolling (not lifting!) head more to get mouth free.

Selected Breathing Drills

1. *Bobbing*
[New drill]

Instr.

Group Management and Safety Tips

This drill should be instituted early in the course and practiced daily, perhaps as a warm-up before class.

Have all students stand in chest- to shoulder-deep water. On command, they breathe at a normal rate, inhaling through their mouth and exhaling through mouth and nose. Continue for about 1 minute. On the second command, they continue the same rhythm but sink underwater to exhale. About 1 minute later, on command, they are to increase the height and depth of the bobbing motion until they are jumping from the bottom and sinking to a full crouch. They may then begin moving about the pool as they bob. Continue for about 5 more minutes without breaking rhythm.

On subsequent use of this drill, you may eliminate the preliminaries. Start your students bobbing from the command ''bobbing: 100 times,'' ''bobbing: 5 minutes,'' or whatever you want.

Watch for students inadvertently bobbing out into deep water, although this exercise can be a future lifesaver if practiced in water a little over standing depth.

Equipment

- None

Instructions to Class

- ''Inhale through your mouth.''
- ''Exhale underwater through nose and mouth.''
- ''Start bobbing 100 times.''

Student Options

- ''Any time you are waiting for a turn or for class to begin, or have any time available, practice bobbing.''
- ''Even in your shower at home, practice mouth inhalation and nose exhalation.''

Student Key to Success

- Steady, even rhythm

Student Success Goal

- Ability to continue easily and indefinitely

To Reduce Difficulty

- Repeat the preliminary stages or stay with them longer.

To Increase Difficulty

- Increase the time or number of bobs.
- Revise the rhythm so your student takes a longer time underwater than above, exhaling at a slow rate and inhaling quickly. Then shift the rhythm so student inhales slowly above water and exhales quickly below.

2. Forward Breathing With Kickboard

[Corresponds to *Swimming*, Step 10, Drill 2]

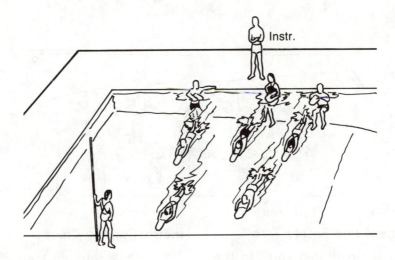

Group Management and Safety Tips

Have students line up with kickboards along the side of the pool in standing depth. Count off for this wave drill so students will be about 3 feet apart (tallest students in deeper water). Demonstrate kicking and breathing forward.

On command, each wave of students should hold their kickboards at arm's length and kick across the pool, exhaling through nose and mouth underwater and inhaling through mouth with the head tipped up so the chin is at water level.

Start the next wave when the preceding one is about 15-20 feet away. Watch carefully that no student inadvertently turns toward deep water.

Equipment

- Kickboards

Instructions to Class

- ''Try to kick all the way across without stopping.''
- ''Breathe to the front. Be sure to exhale fully.''
- ''Number ones ready? Go!''

Student Option

- ''When you reach the other side, practice breathing either while holding the edge or by bobbing until the last wave is finished. Then wait until I call your wave number to start back.''

Student Key to Success

- Steady breathing rhythm with chin at water level

Student Success Goal

- 10 or more consecutive, rhythmical breaths; or kicking across pool width (45 feet) with continuous, rhythmical breathing

To Reduce Difficulty

- Decrease the distance or number of breaths expected. Give selected students two kickboards at first so they can press harder to get chin out.

To Increase Difficulty

- Have swimmer do the drill without a kickboard, using sculling hands (in front) to lift the chin.

3. Bracket and Leg Float, Rhythmic Side Breathing

[Corresponds to *Swimming*, Step 10, Drill 5]

Instr.

Group Management and Safety Tips

Demonstrate rhythmic breathing to the class while holding the pool edge with both hands.

Then have your students line up along the side or end of the pool in the shallow end, with leg floats. Space them about 3 feet apart, ask them to put the leg floats between the knees and both hands on the edge. Have them lay one ear on the water and breathe through the mouth (do not specify which ear; let them choose). Move along the line inspecting the position of each head. Make sure the ear is in the water.

Then ask them to continue to breathe at a normal rate, but to turn the face into the water and exhale through the nose and mouth, then turn up again for the next breath. Continue breathing for 10 breaths, but be sure the ear stays under.

Make individual corrections as they drill. Repeat the drill at least 3 times, until they begin to feel at ease.

Equipment

- Leg floats

Instructions to Class

- "Line up along the side and end about 3 feet apart."
- "Put your leg float between your knees."
- "Hang onto the edge with both hands and let your legs float out."

- "Lay one ear on the water, whichever side feels best, and stay that way, breathing through your mouth only. Let me check to see how you are doing."
- "Now, when I tell you to begin, I want you to turn your face down into the water, exhale through your nose and mouth, and then turn to the side again for the next breath. Be sure to leave your ear under when you turn your head to the side. Take 10 breaths to the side before you stop."
- "Ready? Begin!"

Student Option

- "Turn the head to either side."

Student Key to Success

- Relaxed, easy breathing

Student Success Goal

- Ability to take 10 normal breaths at normal speed without becoming breathless

To Reduce Difficulty

- Give individual attention.
- Reduce the number of consecutive breaths required.

To Increase Difficulty

- Increase the number of breaths required to 20 or 30.

4. Rhythmic Side Breathing, Floating and Kicking

[Corresponds to *Swimming*, Step 10, Drill 7]

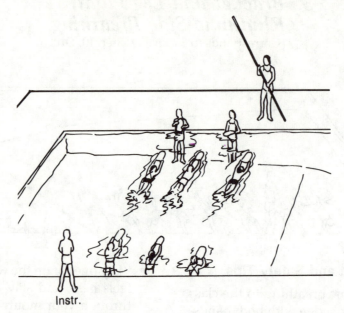

Instr.

Group Management and Safety Tips

Have students line up along the side of the pool in the shallow area. Count off for wave drill so that students in each wave will be about 5 feet apart (usually count by threes or fours). Demonstrate kicking and breathing 10 breaths to the side with a kickboard. Have students perform the drill in waves, stopping after 10 breaths, then starting again until they reach the opposite side.

Start each wave when the preceding wave has completed about 5 breaths. Watch carefully that no one turns inadvertently toward deep water.

Equipment

- Kickboards

Instructions to Class

- "Line up along the side of the pool with a kickboard."
- "Watch me kick and breathe to the side for 10 breaths."
- "Now count off by fours (or whatever)."
- "On command, begin kicking and try to take 10 breaths to the side, then stop and start again until you reach the other side. Be sure your ear stays underwater while

you breathe. Do not lift the head, turn it. If you swallow water, roll farther to get the mouth out higher. You may breathe to either side. Try both sides to see which is easiest."
- "Ones ready? Go!"

Student Option

- "Breathe to either side."

Student Key to Success

- Relaxed, easy breathing with ear underwater

Student Success Goal

- 10 consecutive breaths with ease

To Reduce Difficulty

- Allow the student to pull kickboard closer so he or she can lay ear on board and breathe without turning facedown a few times before doing drill correctly.

To Increase Difficulty

- Have students go all the way across without stopping, taking as many breaths as needed.

Step 11 Pulling and Breathing

This step, a combination of two skills, should not be hurried. Timing breathing to the rhythm of an arm pull is the basis of the crawl stroke, which is the essence of swimming. You may readily assess the proficiency with which your student is getting breaths while pulling. This step ends with a drill that is actually a complete beginner swimming stroke. For that particular drill, you may use the checklist below as a basis for evaluating your student.

Rating the Beginner Stroke, Kick, Pull, and Breathing

CHECKPOINT	BEGINNING LEVEL	NOVICE LEVEL	ACCOMPLISHED LEVEL
Arm Stroke	• Short, hurried, choppy • Arm presses down • Sloppy recovery • Splashes	• Slower, longer pull • Arm pulls back • Smooth recovery though still tense • No glide	• Relaxed, confident • Easy, full pull • Body rolls easily • Recovery, sneaks hand back
Kick	• Foot out of water • Big splash • Knee bent 90 degrees • Much effort	• Feet underwater • Some splash • Knee bent 60 degrees • Some effort	• Smaller kick • Little splash • Flexible knee at 30 degrees • Little effort
Breathing	• Head high, forward • Hesitation • Breathlessness • 1 length maximum swum	• Head to side, ear out • Hesitation • Loud breathing • 2 lengths	• Ear under • Head in line • Smooth roll • Easy breathing • Long distance

Error Detection and Correction for Pulling and Breathing

You should be able to recognize and correct the common problems listed below. The right-hand column lists possible methods for correcting the errors listed in the left column.

ERROR

CORRECTION

1. Swimmer lifts head.

1. Have swimmer repeat Step 11, Drill 4, in *Swimming: Steps to Success*, consisting of supported legs, pulling with one arm, and kickboard in the other hand. Emphasize the ear being under.

2. Student doesn't have enough time to get breath.

2. Emphasize rolling completely onto side and pausing with hand on hip as long as necessary to get breath.

3. Student swims in semi-vertical body position.

3. Caused by a combination of pressing down with hands and raising head. Emphasize pulling back horizontally and keeping ear down.

4. Arm gets in the way of breathing.

4. Student must breathe later, when hand is nearly on thigh.

5. Swimmer is breathless.

5. Usually caused by failing to exhale fully, thereby having stale air remain in lungs.

Selected Pulling and Breathing Drills

1. *Pulling and Breathing With Deep Float, Mask, and Snorkel*

[Corresponds to *Swimming*, Step 11, Drill 1]

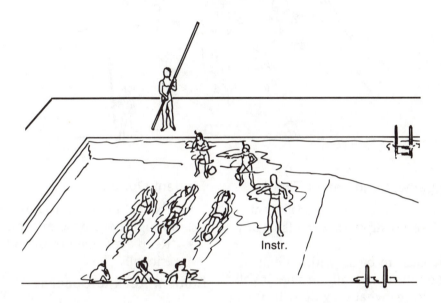

Instr.

Group Management and Safety Tips

It is not useful to demonstrate this drill, because students can't see its underwater components.

Use a wave drill from the side of the shallow area. Each student should have a deep leg float attached to one ankle, and be wearing mask and snorkel. Be alert to students who veer toward deep water. Insist on pulling fully to the thigh, because this becomes important later when the snorkel is set aside.

Equipment

- Deep float leg supports
- Masks and snorkels

Instructions to Class

- ''Be sure to pull all the way through to your thigh.''
- ''Inhale only during the last half of the pull of the breathing-side arm.''
- ''Exhale fully and completely on the pull of the opposite arm.''
- ''Pull and breathe all the way across the pool.''
- ''Ones ready? Go!''

Student Option

- None

Student Keys to Success

- Smooth, full pulls
- No breathlessness

Student Success Goal

- Easy, rhythmic breathing for 10 breaths, or across pool

To Reduce Difficulty

- Shorten the distance required.

To Increase Difficulty

- Have students make a wide turn and continue breathing and stroking on the way back.
- Repeat the drill without masks, but with a snorkel and a band to hold it erect.

2. Pulling and Breathing, No Support

[Corresponds to *Swimming*, Step 11, Drill 5]

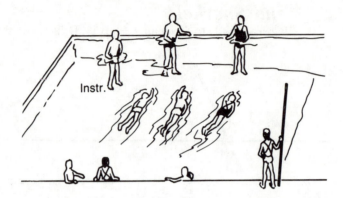

Group Management and Safety Tips

Conduct this wave drill across the shallow area of the pool. Use no supports or aids of any kind.

Instruct the class to begin with an exhalation and pull on the nonbreathing side. It will be interesting to see what they do with their feet. Do not allow them to put conscious effort into kicking. Remind them that downward pressure on the hand will make the feet drop.

Many swimmers tend to keep their eyes closed without a mask, so watch for stragglers who might turn toward deep water.

Equipment

- None

Instructions to Class

- "Pull back—don't press down. Keep your ear under."
- "Roll onto your side; breathe when your arm is alongside your body."
- "Do not kick; let your legs float."
- "Ones ready? Go!"

Student Options

- "Exhale either through nose only or through both nose and mouth."
- "Keep eyes open or open them only occasionally."

Student Keys to Success

- Slow, relaxed strokes
- Full pulls, rolling shoulders fully
- Ear under, head rolled fully during breathing

Student Success Goal

- One easy pool width, or 45 feet

To Reduce Difficulty

- Allow a mask or goggles.

To Increase Difficulty

- Have swimmer breathe on the opposite side.
- Tell your student to count strokes needed to go across pool and try to reduce the number each time.

3. Deep-Water Pull, Kick Breathe, and Turn

[Corresponds to *Swimming*, Step 11, Drill 8]

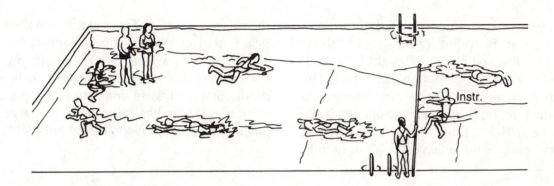

Group Management and Safety Tips

This drill is in effect the major part of the American Red Cross Beginner Swimming Test.

Station yourself in deep water in such a position that the students can swim around you. Have the lifeguard on the side with a reaching pole. Caution the students not to start until you tell them to.

Have the students stand in shallow water near the deep water. Start one at a time; don't start a student until the preceding one is on the way back to shallow water and under the eye of the lifeguard.

Instruct them to start kicking, pulling, and breathing in the shallow area. They should continue into the deep area, turn around you, and continue to the shallow end, swimming between you and the lifeguard.

Equipment

• None

Instructions to Class

• "Do not start until I tell you to."
• "Swim slowly, making full pulls and rolling all the way up for a breath."
• "Swim around me and stay close to the edge on the way back."
• "Heathcliff, ready? Start."

Student Options

• "When your turn comes, you may start at the shallow end and make 2 full pool lengths."
• "You may wear goggles."
• "You may try for a full circuit of the pool perimeter."

Student Key to Success

• Slow, easy, relaxed swimming, with easy breathing and no undue breathlessness

Student Success Goal

• An easy 2 full pool lengths, or 150 feet, of swimming and breathing to the side with confidence

To Reduce Difficulty

• Stay close to reluctant students.
• Have lifeguard trail the reaching pole within reach of the student.
• Allow flotation belt, if necessary.

To Increase Difficulty

• Encourage swimming the pool perimeter.
• Have your student take every other breath on the wrong side. In other words, he or she would breathe on every third arm stroke.

Step 12 Turning Over

Turning over is an interim skill that needs to be taught at this point for reasons of safety. Two turnover methods are taught here: rolling over and passing through the vertical. The turnover through the vertical cannot be taught until the level-off process, both front and back, is learned. The "How To" section of Step 12 in *Swimming: Steps to Success* deals only with the rollover method. Turning through the vertical is part of the drill progressions.

A turnover can be rated entirely on its smoothness and degree of success. It is not productive to classify your student's performance level as to beginner, novice, or accomplished, because this skill is so simple.

Error Detection and Correction for Turning Over

Errors in turning over sometimes result in submersion of the head. This could cause panic in beginners. Common errors are listed below, with possible corrections in the right-hand column.

ERROR	CORRECTION
1. Water gets into nose.	1. Tell student to exhale through the nose as the face turns upward.
2. Body fails to roll over.	2. Several factors need correction: opposite arm extended to side should instead be forward under head; legs apart should be together; top arm needs to reach back; back must arch.
3. Legs drag on the turnover through the vertical (front to back).	3. Have swimmer tuck knees to chin, then press down with both arms extended in front, chin up, head back.
4. Swimmer fails to complete vertical back-to-front turnover.	4. Have swimmer tuck knees tighter and not extend them too soon. Swimmer may have to scoop with his or her hands twice to pull legs back.

Selected Turnover Drills

1. Turnover Drill
[Corresponds to *Swimming*, Step 12, Drill 1]

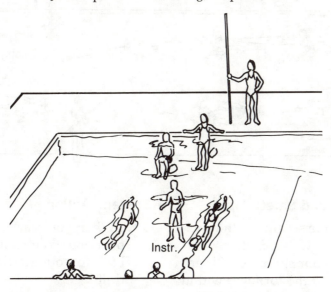

Instr.

Group Management and Safety Tips

Demonstrate the skill using a deep leg support.

Count off for a wave drill so that only two or three are in a wave (divide the number in the class by three, and count off by the resulting number). Use this wave drill in shallow water.

Stay in the water so your students swim toward you. Be alert to slip a hand under the head of any student who appears to be about to submerge (submerging on the back guarantees a noseful).

Equipment

- Deep float leg supports

Instructions to Class

- "When your number is called, pull 3 strokes."
- "On your next breathing-side pull, pull past your hip into the rollover onto your back."
- "Float for 3 breaths, then roll back over and continue across the pool."
- "Number ones ready? Go!"

Student Option

- "Float longer than 3 breaths if you wish before rolling back."

Student Key to Success

- Fluid motions made with confidence

Student Success Goal

- 8-10 turnovers done with ease and confidence

To Reduce Difficulty

- Assist your student's turnover with your hand under his or her head.

To Increase Difficulty

- Have swimmer roll over front to back to front to back to front without stopping.

2. Deep-Water Turnover, Front to Back

[Corresponds to *Swimming*, Step 12, Drill 3]

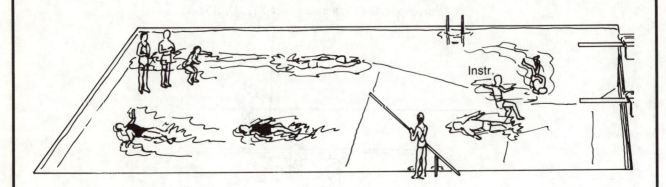

Instr.

Group Management and Safety Tips

Do this drill in single file starting in the shallow area near the deep water. Station yourself in the deep area; your students will turn around you and will do the turnover within reach. Have the lifeguard on the side with a reaching pole. Space the starts so no more than two students are in the deep water at the same time. Demonstrate the skill.

Equipment

- None

Instructions to Class

- ''Do not start until I call you.''
- ''Swim facedown around me, turn over onto your back, and swim to the shallow end on your back.''

Student Option

- ''When you reach the shallow end, turn over onto your stomach again, and swim back to your starting point for the next drill.''

Student Keys to Success

- Self-confidence in ability
- Smoothly regulated movements

Student Success Goal

- 3 round-trips with ease

To Reduce Difficulty

- Stay close to the apprehensive student.

To Increase Difficulty

- Start student at the shallow end to increase the distance.
- Get out of the water so your student feels more on his or her own.

3. Swim and Rest
for Distance
[Corresponds to *Swimming*, Step 12, Drill 6]

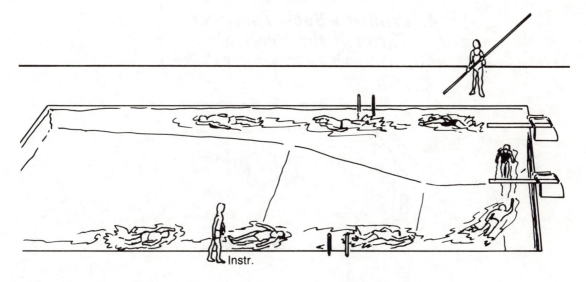

Instr.

Group Management and Safety Tips

Because students swim at different paces and rest for different periods, space is a problem here. It would be best to limit the number of students according to the size of your facility so that they do not bump into each other frequently. You may put lane lines in the pool; have each student assigned to a lane or half a lane. You may wish to have your students swim up one side of the pool, do a wide turn, and swim back on the other side (at least they would all be going in the same direction).

Both you and the lifeguard (and any other helpers you have) should watch very carefully. If you can let only part of the class swim at one time, you should probably limit them to about 200 yards or some time limit before you blow a ''stop'' whistle, so the next group can get a chance. Otherwise, some swimmers may continue all day!

Equipment

- None

Instructions to Class

- ''Swim continuously on your front or back.''
- ''Rest whenever you wish for as long as you wish, but do not touch the bottom or hang onto the side.''
- (Also explain the traffic system.)

Student Option

- ''Choose any stroke and length of resting.''

Student Keys to Success

- Slow, restful strokes
- Easy breathing
- Smooth turnovers

Student Success Goal

- Any distance over 100 yards

To Reduce Difficulty

- Shorten the expected distance.

To Increase Difficulty

- Insist that all swimming be done facedown.

4. Front-to-Back Turnover Through the Vertical
[Corresponds to *Swimming*, Step 12, Drill 7]

Instr.

Group Management and Safety Tips

Demonstrate the skill.

Use a wave drill across the shallow area. Have a wave begin to swim. Then, on a whistle, have them do a vertical turnover and swim back to the wall on their backs. Then start the next wave.

Equipment

- None

Instructions to Class

- "When your number is called, swim out."
- "At the whistle, do a vertical turnover. Tuck your knees tightly to facilitate the turnover."
- "Swim back in on your back."

Student Option

- "Rest for a moment and take a breath before starting to swim back."

Student Keys to Success

- Knees tucked tightly
- Full-arm downward press
- Completely on back before extending legs

Student Success Goal

- 5 or more successful vertical turnovers

Equipment

- None

To Reduce Difficulty

- Stand beside your student to assist.

To Increase Difficulty

- Have your student extend the legs when in a vertical position and level off by kicking the feet up.

5. *Synchronized Vertical Turnover*

[New drill]

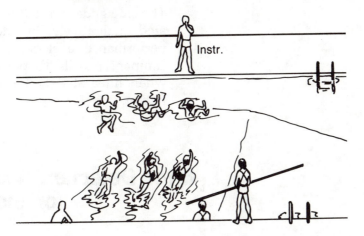

Group Management and Safety Tips

When the class has learned both vertical turnovers (front-to-back and back-to-front), start this wave drill in shallow water.

Teach the class your whistle signals. On the first whistle blast, the first wave starts swimming across the pool. On the second blast they do a quick vertical turnover onto the back. Just as they get onto their back, blow the third blast, which signals them to go back onto the stomach. Simultaneously, at this third blast the second wave starts. Continue this pattern: students turn over on each blast, and a new wave starts on every other blast.

If you let the swimmers stay on the stomach a little longer than on the back, they will make progress across the pool. Tell them to stop when they reach the other side.

Equipment

• None

Instructions to Class

• ''First group start on the first whistle.''
• ''Every whistle means to do a quick vertical turnover, then continue swimming.''
• ''Second group starts on the third whistle, third group starts on the fifth whistle, and so on.''
• ''Stop when you get to the other side.''

Student Option

• None

Student Keys to Success

• Quick, clean turnovers
• No whistles missed

Student Success Goal

• Reach the other side without any collisions

To Reduce Difficulty

• Allow more time between whistles.

To Increase Difficulty

• Make the whistle blasts so close together that the students have little time to do anything but turn over.

Step 13 Side Glide

The side glide is a skill that should be evaluated qualitatively, but does not warrant a performance level rating. In fact, it and its companion skills disappear as separate skills when integrated to form a unified combination.

Error Detection and Correction for the Side Glide

Your students will discover new errors to commit, but the typical errors listed below may be corrected by the actions listed in the right-hand column.

ERROR 🚫 | **CORRECTION**

ERROR	CORRECTION
1. Student rolls onto stomach.	1. Have student straighten hips, arch back just a bit more, move top arm a little farther back, and lift chin a little so head is tilted slightly back.
2. Student rolls onto back.	2. Swimmer should move top arm forward a bit, bend slightly forward at hips, drop chin a little, turn face into water, and hold breath. Swimmer should not turn shoulder.
3. Body sinks.	3. Give nonbuoyant persons a float belt for this skill until enough forward speed can be obtained to compensate for lack of buoyancy. Most students, though, need only to take bigger breaths.

Selected Side Glide Drills

1. Side Glide From Push-Off With Leg Support

[Corresponds to *Swimming*, Step 13, Drill 1]

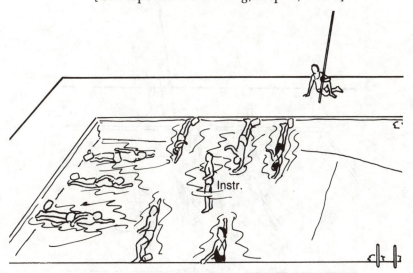

Group Management and Safety Tips

Be sure to demonstrate the skill, including all the errors and corrections, so your students can see the effects of correcting moves. You can be of more help if you are in the water with them during their drilling.

There is not enough forward movement in this skill to use a wave drill. Students should be spaced around the walls of the shallow area. Be careful to place them far enough from the corners that they do not collide with each other on the push-off. Be sure only one foot is in the deep float loop; thus, they can get a foot on the bottom when they wish. They may start simultaneously or practice on their own as you walk around helping individually.

Equipment

- Deep leg floats for all
- Float belts for nonbuoyant students

Instructions to Class

- "With one foot in the deep float loop, one hand on the pool edge, and the other pointing out into the pool, lay your ear on your forward arm and push off on your side."
- "Take a big breath and hold it."

- "Balance yourself in a side glide position."
- "Breathe quickly and hold each breath."

Student Options

- "Nonbuoyant persons may wear a float belt, if necessary."
- "Take the leg float off if you don't need it."

Student Keys to Success

- Patience
- Practice
- Sense of balance

Student Success Goal

- A balanced side glide position held for 30 seconds or more

To Reduce Difficulty

- Give individual help.
- Allow a kickboard under the *top* arm for the first trial or two.

To Increase Difficulty

- Don't allow a leg float.
- Make a longer time requirement.
- Have your student push off from the bottom.

2. *Pull and Side Glide, Breathing Side Only*
[Corresponds to *Swimming*, Step 13, Drill 4]

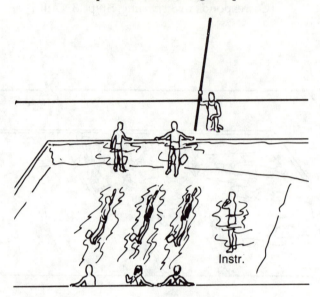

Instr.

Group Management and Safety Tips

Demonstrate the skill.

Use a wave drill across the shallow area. Insist on 4 seconds in each side float, but more than that is not useful. It is not necessary to wait until the third stroke to begin the side floats, but it gives time to think.

Be alert for students pulling into deep water.

Equipment

- Deep float leg supports for each student

Instructions to Class

- "When your number is called, with the deep leg float attached, push off the side and start to pull."
- "After 2 or 3 pulls, turn up into a side float for 4 seconds (count to yourself), but only on your breathing side."
- "Stop and float in side position every time breathing-side arm pulls. Inhale during the float. Be sure to count four before continuing."
- "Ones ready? Go!"

Student Option

- "Do without a leg float."

Student Keys to Success

- Full arm pulls
- Body semirelaxed in float position
- Breathing easily during float

Student Success Goal

- 5 consecutive side glides of 4 seconds each

To Reduce Difficulty

- Give individual help in the water.

To Increase Difficulty

- Have student go all the way across the pool.
- Don't allow leg float.
- Make swimmer hold the float for 5 seconds or more.

3. Hesitation Side Glide
[Corresponds to *Swimming*, Step 13, Drill 7]

Instr.

Group Management and Safety Tips

This drill prepares the student for the over-hand stroke. It should be repeated until it is very easy to do.

Use a wave drill across the shallow area first. Then, if student progress warrants, run the drill from end to end, including deep water. Instruct the students to pause for 2 seconds only in a side glide position at the end of each arm pull, meanwhile using a small kick and breathing rhythmically on one side.

Equipment

- Goggles optional

Instructions to Class

- ''When your number is called, swim in a prone position across the pool with a side glide stop of 2 seconds after each arm pull.''
- ''Ones ready? Go!''

Student Option

- None

Student Keys to Success

- Long, full pulls
- Relaxed, easy glides
- Rhythmical breathing

Student Success Goal

- 10 or more smooth, easy strokes with a short, restful pause after each stroke

To Reduce Difficulty

- Shorten the distance required.
- Allow masks and snorkels.

To Increase Difficulty

- Have student swim lengths, including deep water.
- Tell swimmer to breathe on both sides.
- Set a goal of 100 yards.

Step 14   Overhand Arm Stroke

The overhand arm stroke is the most visible part of the crawl stroke. Using the arm stroke as a focal point, it is easy to classify swimmers into categories. The chart below can aid you in such a rating.

Overhand Arm Stroke Rating

CHECKPOINT	BEGINNING LEVEL	NOVICE LEVEL	ACCOMPLISHED LEVEL
Recovery	• Shoulder low • Hand leads elbow • Wrist bent back • Stiff, awkward	• Rolls more • Elbow first • Palm down, hurried • Wrist straight • Tense	• Shoulder high • Palm up • Elbow high • Fingers trail • Wrist relaxed • Hand relaxed
Entry	• Elbow first • Shoulder down • Elbow bent • Short reach • Stiff, awkward • Splash • No glide	• Arm flat • Wrist straight • Elbow bent • Shoulder down too soon • Not stretched • No glide • Short reach	• ''Over barrel'' • Elbow high • Fingers first • Shoulder up • Wrist relaxed • Stretch forward • Glide (catch) • Smooth, fluid
Pull	• Elbow leads • Forearm flat • Short • Hand out at waist • Quick • Wrist hooked	• Arm straight, presses down • Wrist straight • Hand out at hip • Stiff, tight • Rolls late • Pulls wide	• Elbow high • Wrist flexes • Pull along centerline • Elbow bent 90 degrees • Rolls early • Pulls to thigh • Long pull • Effective

Error Detection and Correction for the Overhand Stroke

Actually, only the above-water part of this stroke is new. The pull has not changed from the underwater-recovery stroke the student has been doing. However, when the overhand recovery is introduced, errors may creep into the entire stroke. The list below identifies errors you should catch, and the right-hand column suggests corrections.

ERROR

CORRECTION

1. Pull is too short.

1. Have student pull until thumb touches thigh below bathing suit.

2. Hand is palm down on recovery.

2. Have student rotate arm at shoulder to turn palm up and try to flex wrist so hand "holds water" all the way to face. With wrist flexed, fingertips should turn to point outward.

3. Hand and arm are lifted high out of water.

3. Tell swimmer to relax wrist, trail fingertips in water on recovery.

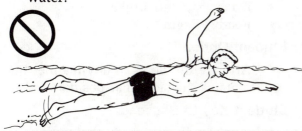

4. Elbow is low on entry, or elbow enters before fingers.

4. Emphasize side glide position and holding side glide until fingertips touch water, *then* rolling down arm "over barrel."

5. Entry is short, with no reach.

5. Have student stretch and reach over *bigger* "barrel."

Selected Overhand Arm Stroke Drills

1. Overhand Drill, Breathing Side, Supported
[Corresponds to *Swimming*, Step 14, Drill 1]

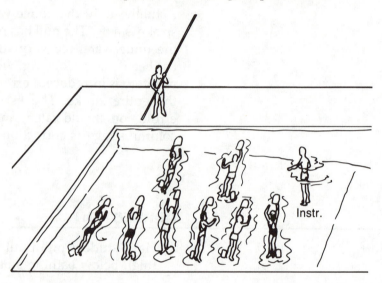

Group Management and Safety Tips

Very little forward progress is expected on this drill. Therefore, a wave drill may not work. Try spreading the class out in the shallow area so each student has room to float and move forward a little.

Emphasize this is just floating and slow motion recovery; no pull is expected. Allow students, using a deep leg float and kickboard, to hold kickboard (or two) like a violin if it works better.

Demonstrate the skill. Show both methods for holding the kickboard. Call out the important points as you move about through the students and make corrections.

Equipment

- Deep float leg supports
- Kickboards

Instructions to Class

- "Spread out."
- "Use leg float and kickboard, float in side glide position."
- "S-L-O-W-L-Y recover top arm in overhand stroke recovery."
- "Listen to important points as I call them out to you."
- "Do not pull; just let your arm slip gently through the water."
- "Do at least ten strokes."
- "Ready? Begin!"

Student Option

- "Arrange the floats in any manner that facilitates the side float position."

Student Key to Success

- Move slowly and study the motion

Student Success Goal

- 10 or more recoveries in good form

To Reduce Difficulty

- Allow additional support.
- Give individual attention.

To Increase Difficulty

- Selectively remove supports.
- Require forward movement.

2. "Touch-and-Go" Overhand Stroke Drill, Leg Support

[Corresponds to *Swimming*, Step 14, Drill 4]

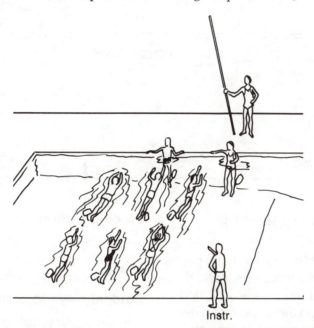

Instr.

Group Management and Safety Tips

Use deep float leg supports. Use a wave drill across the shallow water area. Demonstrate the drill. Emphasize full pulls, full breaths, and actual touching of the forward hand in "touch-and-go." Stress holding full side glide position until hand is just about to touch forward hand.

Equipment

- Leg floats

Instructions to Class

- "When your number is called, pull across the pool using 'touch-and-go,' full pulls, full breaths, and stay on your side until the recovering hand is about to touch the forward hand."

Student Option

- Go without float

Student Keys to Success

- Attain side glide position on every arm stroke
- Use full arm pulls

Student Success Goal

- 10 or more consecutive arm strokes in good form

To Reduce Difficulty

- Give individual attention.

To Increase Difficulty

- Have student remove the leg float.
- Add a turn requirement.

3. Deep-Water Overhand Stroke for Distance

[Corresponds to *Swimming*, Step 14, Drill 9]

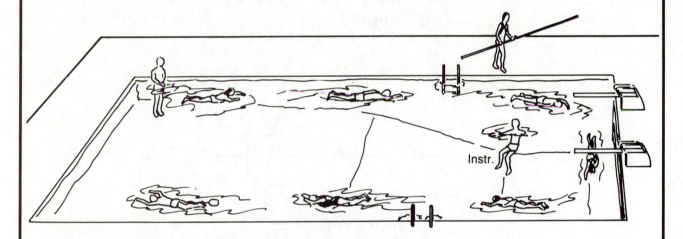

Instr.

Group Management and Safety Tips

Demonstrate the turn.

Start your students at the corner of the pool at the shallow end. Have them swim along the wall out to the deep end, across the deep end, and back down the opposite pool wall. Then start at the opposite corner so the turns must be made in the opposite direction.

Have the lifeguard at the deep end with reaching pole. Start the students in single file, at intervals large enough that only two or three are in deep water at one time. Stay in the deep water to supervise. Use no equipment except goggles, if students wish.

Equipment

- Goggles, if desired

Instructions to Class

- ''Do not start until I start you.''
- ''Swim out along this wall, turn, swim across the deep end, and back down the other wall to the shallow end.''
- ''Use the overhand stroke all the way and go slow and easy with full pulls.''

Student Option

- ''When you reach the shallow end, continue to swim, turn, and swim across to the starting point.''

Student Keys to Success

- Slow, easy, full pulls
- Full breaths
- Adequate shoulder roll

Student Success Goal

- Swim continuously for more than 2 pool lengths in good form

To Reduce Difficulty

- Have student cut the turn short to reduce the distance.
- Start swimmer at midpool to reduce the distance.

To Increase Difficulty

- Add a fourth leg across the shallow end.
- Have student go 2 full circles around the pool.

Step 15   Crawl Stroke

It is almost impossible to watch someone swim the crawl stroke without judging him or her on the stroke. Poor swimmers are evident, mediocre swimmers are numerous, and accomplished swimmers are a joy to watch. The following table rates the stroke performance level according to three important stroke components.

Crawl Stroke Rating

CHECKPOINT	BEGINNING LEVEL	NOVICE LEVEL	ACCOMPLISHED LEVEL
Kick	• Lower leg only, "pedaling," or "pumping" • Foot hooked • Splashing • Two beats	• Tense, rigid • Knees stiff • Ankles stiff • Toes pointed • Small flutter • Too fast • Ragged rhythm	• Relaxed • From hip • Knees flex • Ankles flop • Up and down • Six beats • Rhythmic
Body and Head Position	• Head up, looking forward • Ears out • Feet low • Little roll • Rising and sinking	• Ear in • Rolls more to breathing side • Rising to breathe • Breathing late	• Horizontal • Equal roll • Rhythmic roll • Breathing early
Arms	• Tense, tight • Presses down • Short pull • Elbow low • Palm down • Fingers lead	• Long pull • Wide pull • Erratic beat • High recovery • Arm flat • Elbow straight	• Pull down center-line • Elbow high "over barrel," bent 90 degrees • Fingers trail • Six beats

Error Detection and Correction for the Crawl Stroke

The most obvious errors applicable here have been covered in Step 11 (Pulling and Breathing) and Step 14 (Overhand Arm Stroke). Common errors in kicking and coordination are listed below, with suggestions in the right-hand column on how they may be corrected.

ERROR 🚫

CORRECTION

ERROR	CORRECTION
1. Swimmer kicks from knees only.	1. Overcorrect by asking for totally straight knees (temporary measure).
2. Swimmer pumps or pedals.	2. Guide legs by hand in bracket drill.
3. Knees or ankles are stiff.	3. Stress relaxation. Have student kick on both front and back with fins.
4. Swimmer kicks 2 or 4 beats per stroke.	4. Don't correct this if it seems easy and natural. It's acceptable.
5. Swimmer kicks 8 or 10 beats per stroke.	5. Overcorrect by asking student not to kick at all, but to let relaxed legs drag. Student will probably fall into a naturally slower coordination upon resumption of kick.

Selected Crawl Stroke Drills

1. Crawl Stroke Kick Drill

[Corresponds to *Swimming*, Step 15, Drill 1]

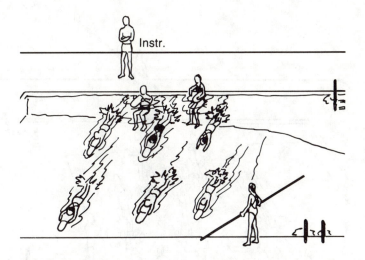

Group Management and Safety Tips

Demonstrate the kick, counting out loud and making a definite splash on counts 1 and 4, overemphasizing for effect.

Use a wave drill with kickboards across the shallow area. Keep in mind the fact that we teach a 6-beat kick but later accept a 2- or 4-beat kick if it seems more natural. No more than 6 beats is acceptable, though, because the effort is not worth the propulsion. Stress kicking from the hip, not the knee, and keeping the knee flexible. The ankle must be loose and floppy.

Equipment

- Kickboards

Instructions to Class

- "Hold the kickboard at arm's length in both hands."
- "When your number is called, kick across the pool. Kick from the hips. Let your ankles flop and count kicks in sets of 6. Start counting with the leg on the breathing side and emphasize the 1 and 4 beats."
- "Ones ready? Go!"

Student Option

- None

Student Keys to Success

- Controlled knee bend and floppy ankle
- Stop and restart if count is lost

Student Success Goal

- 1 pool width, or 45 feet, kicking correctly and with count

To Reduce Difficulty

- Work on the student's kick only before introducing the counting.
- Recommend bracket drill and guide student's legs by hand before regular drilling.

To Increase Difficulty

- Have swimmer speed up the kick without losing count.

2. Crawl Kick With Swim Fins, Kickboard, Breathing Side Pull

[New drill]

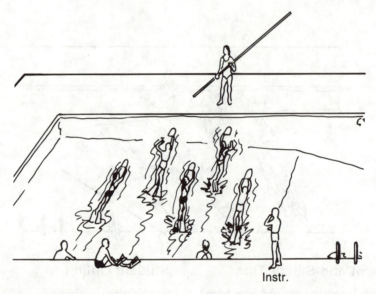

Instr.

Group Management and Safety Tips

Use a wave drill across the shallow area. Demonstrate the drill as follows: wear swim fins. Hold the kickboard at arm's length in the non-breathing-side hand. Your breathing-side hand should be alongside the kickboard with the thumb resting on the board.

Start the crawl kick, counting 1 on the breathing-side leg. After a complete set of 6 kicks, start pulling with the breathing-side arm and roll to the side glide position on the 4 count. Inhale on the 5 and 6 counts. Roll down and return the hand to the kickboard on the 1 count. Exhale on the 2 and 3 count and repeat the cycle.

Continue the one-armed swim across the pool.

Equipment

- Swim fins
- Kickboards

Instructions to Class

- "When your number is called, swim across the pool using breathing-side arm only, as demonstrated."
- "Take your time; long pulls; side position for breathing."
- "Ones ready? Go!"

Student Option

- None

Student Keys to Success

- Deliberate motions
- Think carefully through each part

Student Success Goal

- 1 pool width, or 45 feet, of correct performance

To Reduce Difficulty

- Have swimmer bring the kickboard in under the forward arm, lay the ear on the forward arm, and keep the face to the side, mouth out, all the time.

To Increase Difficulty

- It's hard enough already.

3. "Hesitation" Crawl Stroke

[Corresponds to *Swimming*, Step 15, Drill 7]

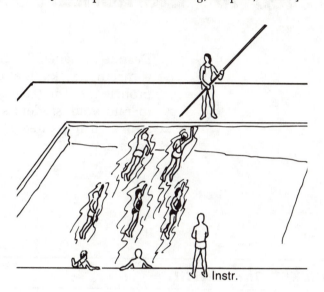

Instr.

Group Management and Safety Tips

This drill is very important. It integrates the side glide position, fixes the time of breathing, and ingrains the fact that floating is an integral part of swimming. It fosters relaxation during swimming.

Use a wave drill across the shallow area. Repeat it until all are swimming slowly, restfully, and gracefully.

Equipment

- Goggles, if student wishes

Instructions to Class

- "Swim a slow crawl stroke across the pool."
- "Turn up into a side glide position on *each* side and pause for a 2-second count before continuing. Breathe on one side only, keep the face in the water on the opposite side."
- "Slow. Easy. Relaxed."
- "Ones ready? Go!"

Student Option

- None.

Student Keys to Success

- Slow speed
- Breath control
- Body balance in the side position

Student Success Goal

- Minimum of 10 strokes correctly (but real success is ability to continue indefinitely)

To Reduce Difficulty

- Do not insist on a 6-beat kick.

To Increase Difficulty

- Do not increase the difficulty.

Step 16 Elementary Backstroke

Despite its name, the elementary backstroke is a complex skill that can be rated as to its proficiency. The table below can enable you to rate your student's performance of the stroke, using three stroke components as criteria.

Elementary Backstroke Rating

CHECKPOINT	BEGINNING LEVEL	NOVICE LEVEL	ACCOMPLISHED LEVEL
Kick	• Knees out of water • One or both feet pointed • Sitting position • One knee in	• Knees under • Toes hooked, not turned out • Narrow kick • One foot turned inward • Hips level	• Knees under • Toes hooked • Toes turned out • Wide kick • Hips level • Powerful drive
Arm Pull	• Short pull • Ends late • Short recovery • No reach for catch • Not level	• Reaches higher • Pulls longer • Full recovery • No reach for catch • Narrow	• High reach • Stretches for catch • Wide, full pull • Level pull • Ends with kick
Body Position and Coordination	• Sitting • Pull ends late • Rises, falls • Splash • No glide	• Level, hips up • Pull ends late • Rises, falls • No splash • Some glide	• Horizontal • Pull, kick end simultaneously • Rides level • Long glide

Error Detection and Correction for the Backstroke

Rating a stroke requires detection of errors, but you also need to know how to correct them. The table below suggests in the right-hand column how to correct the errors listed to the left.

ERROR

CORRECTION

1. Toes are not pointed out.

1. With student in bracket position, guide the feet through the motion by hand. With student free-floating with a kickboard, place hands on inside of ankles and have student push against hands.

2. Student swims in sitting position.

2. With student floating on back with kickboard, hold your hand under small of student's back and lift while student drops heels back under.

3. Body rises and sinks.

3. Demonstrate the cause (arm pulling downward, not level pull); exaggerate the fault, making face go under, to show student the result of the error.

4. Water washes over face on recovery.

4. Demonstrate the cause. Have student pull while on the back to get water on the top of the body moving. Then bring knees up and make lots of resistance on the arm recovery, stopping the body suddenly. Water will continue moving—right into the student's face. Raise the chin so water breaks around chin instead of going over the face.

Selected Elementary Backstroke Drills

1. Elementary Backstroke Kick, Land Drill

[Corresponds to *Swimming*, Step 16, Drill 1]

Instr.

Group Management and Safety Tips

Have the students sit on the edge of the pool with their legs hanging over the edge from midthigh. Use the sides and ends of the pool in the shallow area. Space them so that when feet are spread, they do not kick their neighbors. Use a "drill on command."

Equipment

- None

Instructions to Class

- "Lean back on your elbows, and kick *only on command*."
- "Feet together, knees straight." (When everyone is in position, give the next command.)
- "Drop your heels down behind you and hook your feet." (Walk around to check that all feet are hooked. [In deck-level pools, the feet will be underwater.])
- "Turn your feet so the hooked toes point out to the sides." (Have them hold the position until you can check it.)
- "Move your feet out to the sides, but keep your toes hooked. Let your knees separate." (Once again, check the position.)
- "With the inside of the foot and ankle, push water out and around, and squeeze your feet together, toes still hooked."
- "Now point your toes."
- Have everyone stay together and drill on command as you walk around looking for errors.
- Say, "Heels back." "Toes hooked." "Toes turn out." "Out, around, and drive." "Toes point." Continue to call the commands as you help individuals correct errors.

Student Option

- "Continue to kick on your own while I watch for errors."

Student Keys to Success

- Kick together with class on command
- Learn concept that the push comes from the inside of the foot and ankle

Student Success Goal

- Kick correctly with class in land drill

To Reduce Difficulty

- Give individual help.
- Reduce the drill time.

To Increase the Difficulty

- Do not increase the difficulty.

2. Backstroke Kick Drill, Kickboard on Chest

[Corresponds to *Swimming*, Step 16, Drill 4]

Group Management and Safety Tips

Demonstrate the drill.

Caution class against holding the kickboard too tightly against chest. The hips have to have a little leeway to drop slightly on the thrust.

Use a wave drill across the shallow area. Stay in the water to aid those who need it. Then get up on the deck for awhile so you can see better.

Equipment

- Kickboards

Instructions to Class

- "When your wave is called, hold your kickboard slightly away from your chest and kick across the pool."
- "Kick solidly and glide long."
- "Ones ready? Go!"

Student Option

- None

Student Keys to Success

- Push with the inside of the ankle
- Feet lead knees outward in a wide kick

Student Success Goal

- 20-45 feet of forward progress

To Reduce Difficulty

- Use the shorter distance goal.
- Give individual attention.

To Increase Difficulty

- Require a longer distance goal.
- Eliminate kickboard use.

3. Coordinated Elementary Backstroke
[Corresponds to *Swimming*, Step 16, Drill 6]

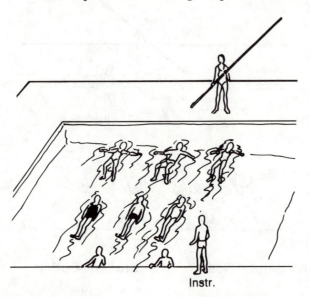

Instr.

Group Management and Safety Tips

Demonstrate the coordinated elementary backstroke in slow motion, calling attention to the various elements.

Use a wave drill across the shallow area.

Equipment

- None

Instructions to Class

- "As your number is called, do a back float, then start a very slow elementary backstroke."
- "Feet drop, hook, turn out, and drive out and around."
- "Arms slide up, turn out, reach, and pull."

Student Option

- None

Student Keys to Success

- Long pulls with simultaneous wide kicks
- Long glide

Student Success Goal

- 10 or more full pulls and simultaneous kicks with long glides

To Reduce Difficulty

- Have your student slow down and use stop-motion techniques to think through the skill.

To Increase Difficulty

- Have swimmers compete for distance per stroke.

4. Elementary Backstroke for Distance
[Corresponds to *Swimming*, Step 16, Drill 9]

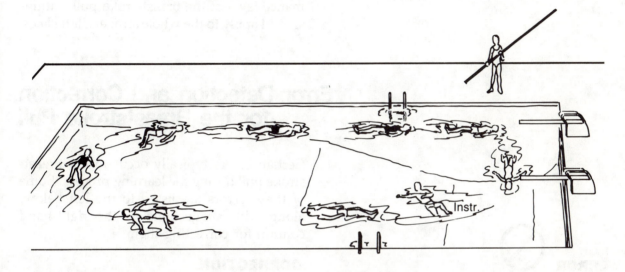

Group Management and Safety Tips

This drill involves deep water, so the students should go single file with separation that allows only a few in the deep area at one time. To minimize midpool collisions, it would be best to have the students start at a corner in the shallow end, go single file to the deep end with separation, turn across the pool, and come back on the other side. Continue these full circles of the pool perimeter until desired distance has been achieved.

Post the lifeguard at one part of the deep area. You patrol the other part.

Equipment

- None

Instructions to Class

- "Wait until I start you, then swim elementary backstroke twice around the pool, staying close to the edge."
- "Swim slowly, long pulls, long glides."
- "Be alert to others to avoid collisions."

Student Option

- "You may turn over, or partly over, occasionally to relieve the boredom and to see who is in front of you."

Student Keys to Success

- Easy, full strokes
- Long glides

Student Success Goal

- 2 full circles around the pool, or at least 100 yards

To Reduce Difficulty

- Reduce the distance required.
- Allow sculling for part of the distance.

To Increase Difficulty

- Increase the distance required.
- Have the class turn over on signal and swim some of the distance in crawl stroke.

Step 17 Breaststroke Pull

Little progress through the water is made using the breaststroke pull alone. All your effort should be directed toward the student's correct arm placement and movement patterns.

It is not practical to try to rate the performance level of the breaststroke pull: ratings should apply to the whole stroke, a little later.

Error Detection and Correction for the Breaststroke Pull

Certain errors typically occur in the breaststroke pull during the learning process. Some of these errors are listed to the left below, along with suggestions in the right-hand column for correcting them.

ERROR   **CORRECTION**

ERROR	CORRECTION
1. Swimmer pulls out to side with elbows straight.	1. Emphasize that the first movements of the pull are to flex the wrists, and bend the elbows, so that the hands and forearms are pointing straight down, before starting to pull from shoulders.
2. Swimmer pulls too far.	2. Compare the pull to an eggbeater. Hands and forearms, pointing down, are the beaters. They make counter-rotating circles *in front of the face*. They never even reach chin level until elbows come in at the end of the pull. Hands stay at chin level while elbows come in. Hands never pull past shoulders.
3. Head, shoulders, and chest come out of water during inhalation.	3. Arms are wrongly pressing *down* to lift shoulders. Instead, they should only press *back*. Have student practice floating, arms in front, and tilting the chin up forward just to water level. This shows student that downward pressure is not necessary to get mouth out of water.

Selected Breaststroke Pull Drills

1. Breaststroke Pull, Land Drill
[New drill]

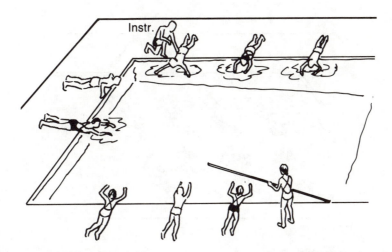

Group Management and Safety Tips

Arrange the students around the perimeter of the pool on the deck with at least 4 feet between them. Have them lie on their stomachs perpendicular to the pool edge, their bodies extended out over the water so their arms hang straight down along the pool wall. (If a gutter is uncomfortable, it can sometimes be bridged or filled with kickboards or mats.)

In this position, use a "drill-on-command" technique to go through the motions of the breaststroke pull. It allows you to see the arms and hands but is uncomfortable if continued too long (unsupported head). Walk around the pool deck making corrections.

Equipment

- Kickboards or mats to lie on

Instructions to Class

- "Lie down on the deck with your head out over the water, with arms hanging straight down along the wall."
- "Stay with my commands; don't get ahead of me."

- "Stretch out your arms, flex your wrists, turn out your palms, bend your elbows until forearms point down, pull back to wall, turn palms in, slide hands along wall to chin, palms down, push arms out in front, glide."

Student Option

- None

Student Key to Success

- Stay together with others on commands

Student Success Goal

- 10 land drill strokes

To Reduce Difficulty

- Reduce the number of strokes practiced.

To Increase Difficulty

- Have student extend farther over the water so the elbows can be brought in at the end of the stroke.
- Increase the number of strokes.

2. Slow-Motion Breaststroke Pulls

[Corresponds to *Swimming*, Step 17, Drill 1]

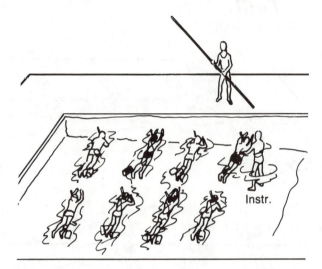

Instr.

Group Management and Safety Tips

There is not enough forward motion in this drill to use a wave pattern. Arrange students in rows across the shallow area with a little space in front to allow for *some* movement. They should have space to stretch arms out without touching.

Demonstrate the drill in extreme slow motion. You might even use a "drill-on-command" technique, calling out the positional and movement commands: "stretch; flex wrists; bend elbows, elbows high; forearms point down; palms turn out, pull out, around, and in to chin; elbows in; thrust arms forward; glide." Wander among the class, making corrections as you go.

Equipment

- Masks and snorkels
- Leg floats

Instructions to Class

- "Using mask, snorkel, and leg float, float and breathe in prone position."
- "Stay with my commands for the first 2 strokes, then continue in *extreme* slow motion through the breaststroke pull. Try not to go forward—just make the arm movements."
- "Do at least 10 strokes."
- "I'll be around to watch."

Student Option

- "Use 'pull-buoys' instead of deep leg supports."

Student Keys to Success

- *Extreme* slow motion
- Individual help

Student Success Goal

- 10 or more correct stroke patterns

To Reduce Difficulty

- Provide float belts for the nonbuoyant.

To Increase Difficulty

- Don't allow use of leg support.
- Increase the number of strokes required.

3. Coordinated Breaststroke Breathing

[Corresponds to *Swimming*, Step 17, Drill 4]

Instr.

Group Management and Safety Tips

Demonstrate the drill.

Use a wave drill across the shallow area. Emphasize quick, hard pulls for forward propulsion, because the power of the pull supports the head lift for breathing. Caution the students against holding the head up for more than an instant to get the breath, because holding the head up too long inevitably results in pulling past the shoulder level.

Equipment

- Leg floats
- Goggles, if desired

Instructions to Class

- "When your wave is called, with your leg support, pull and breathe across the pool."
- "Start lifting your head at the start of the pull. Inhale on the last half of the pull, keeping your chin on the water, and drop your head back into the water immediately."
- "Exhale on the glide."
- "Ones ready? Go!"

Student Options

- "Go without the float if you wish."
- "You may wear goggles if you wish."

Student Keys to Success

- Get the feel of the power portion of the pull
- Stay low in the water on inhalation

Student Success Goal

- 20 consecutive pulls with correct breathing

To Reduce Difficulty

- Require fewer practice strokes.
- Allow float belts.

To Increase Difficulty

- Don't allow use of leg floats.
- Require breathing on every second stroke, head remaining down on others. This requires more breath control.
- Do not urge trying for more distance per stroke. This would result in pulling past the shoulder.

Step 18   Breaststroke

The breaststroke is a combination of individual skills into a package that is one of the strokes recognized by competitive swimming organizations. Students typically display a variety of skill levels, even within the same class. Three stroke components have been selected to indicate the variances in techniques swum by beginners, novices, and accomplished swimmers. You may use these criteria as an evaluation tool if you wish.

Breaststroke Rating

CHECKPOINT	BEGINNING LEVEL	NOVICE LEVEL	ACCOMPLISHED LEVEL
Arm Stroke	• Too wide • To waist • Presses down • Elbows straight • Wrists rigid	• Weak • Slightly wide • Past shoulders • Presses down • Elbows bent 110 degrees • Wrists flex	• Powerful • Circular pull to shoulders • Pulls back • Elbows bent 90 degrees • Forearms point down • Wrists flex
Kick	• Toes point • Knees too wide • Knee turns in • Feet not turned out • Knees under body • No squeeze	• One toe points • One knee in • One foot turns out • Feet up • Hips straight • Squeezes	• Feet hooked • Feet turn out • Knees narrow • Powerful drive • Hips straight • Squeezes • Streamlined
Body Position and Coordination	• Rises, falls • Lifts too high • Simultaneous pull, kick • No glide • Kicks before pull • Keeps head up	• Rises, falls • Lifts some • Pulls before kick • Short glide • Head submerges • Kicks late • Breathes early	• Rides level • Chin to water level • Pull, kick, glide • Long glide • Breathes at end of stroke • Head to eyebrow level

Error Detection and Correction for the Breaststroke

Many errors can creep into the complex coordination of the breaststroke. The table below lists some common breaststroke errors in the left-hand column, with some possible corrective measures in the right-hand column.

ERROR 🚫   **CORRECTION**

ERROR	CORRECTION
1. Swimmer kicks before pulling.	1. This usually occurs when glide is omitted. Have student say "pull, kick, glide" silently while doing so. Have student "kick" arms into glide position.
2. Swimmer fails to glide.	2. Have student hold kickboard in both hands, release the board to take a stroke, then thrust the hands forward to catch the board again.
3. Kick is late.	3. Make sure that heels are recovering *during* the pull, not after.
4. Body rises and falls.	4. Caused by hands being flat on the water and pressing downward during the pull. Be sure swimmer holds hands and forearms vertical, digs in with fingertips to start pull, and keeps elbows high in "over the barrel" position.
5. Head submerges on glide.	5. Have swimmer keep chin up to look forward, not down, during glide.
6. One knee turns in, one foot points, creating a scissors kick.	6. This illegal kick is a common fault. Reteach the breaststroke kick.

Selected Breaststroke Drills

1. Breaststroke Kick, Bracket Drill

[Corresponds to *Swimming*, Step 18, Drill 1]

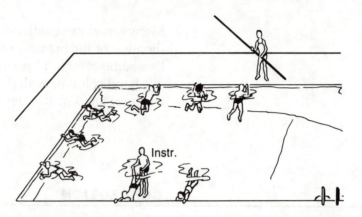

Instr.

Group Management and Safety Tips

Devote extra time to this drill, because this kick is the most difficult to learn and must be learned well.

After reviewing the kick on the back, have students bracket on the pool edge around the shallow area. Allow sufficient spacing to avoid kicking each other on a wide kick. Have them bracket by placing one hand on the pool edge and the other *directly* beneath it, palm against the wall, fingertips pointing straight down. They should pull gently on the top hand and press gently with the lower hand. Their feet can be held at a position about 18-20 inches underwater, with the bodies straight. If a student's body tends to swing to one side or the other, he or she should move the bottom hand slightly in the same direction until a steady position can be held.

Stay in the water and walk behind the students, ready to guide erring feet. Use a "drill on command," calling the commands at first with spacing so you can check positions, then with increasing speed for practice.

Equipment

- None

Instructions to Class

- "Bracket. Stay together, hold each position until I ask for the next."
- "Ready? Heels up; hold."
- "Ankles hooked; hold."
- "Toes pointed out; hold."
- "Feet move out. Keep knees fairly close."
- "Drive out and around; squeeze."
- "Toes point. Hold the glide."

Thereafter:
- "Heels up and hooked."
- "Toes out."
- "Drive and squeeze."

Student Option

- None

Student Keys to Success

- Exact, precise movements
- Repetition

Student Success Goal

- Feel the pressure on the inside of the foot and ankle

To Reduce Difficulty

- Do not insist on thrusting hard and fast, but only on correct positions.
- Maintain a slow-motion drill.

To Increase Difficulty

- Do not increase difficulty.

2. *Breaststroke Kick With Kickboard*

[Corresponds to *Swimming*, Step 18, Drill 3]

Group Management and Safety Tips

Demonstrate the drill.

Use a wave drill across the shallow area. Each student should hold a kickboard at arm's length. Insist more on correct motions than on forward progress.

Stand on the pool deck for better visibility, but don't hesitate to get in and guide a student's legs by hand if needed.

Equipment

- Kickboards
- Goggles at students' discretion

Instructions to Class

- "When your number is called, push off the wall and do the breaststroke kick across the pool."
- "Lift your chin to breathe and drop your face in to exhale."
- "Long glide, please."

Student Option

- "Keep your head up all the time if it aids concentration on the kick."

Student Keys to Success

- Conscious thought to each leg position
- Slow, thoughtful recovery with powerful thrust

Student Success Goal

- 1 pool width kicking correctly, or 45 feet

To Reduce Difficulty

- Allow student to pull kickboard back under arms so chin rests on board.

To Increase Difficulty

- Have your student count kicks to increase distance per kick.
- Increase the distance required.

3. Breaststroke Coordination With Mask, Snorkel

[Corresponds to *Swimming*, Step 18, Drill 4]

Instr.

Group Management and Safety Tips

Even though you stress doing this drill in very slow motion without thought of forward progress, there will be forward motion, primarily from the kick. Therefore, a wave drill across the shallow area works well.

Demonstrate this drill, calling specific attention to the relationship of the arms to the legs at various points in the stroke.

Masks and snorkels allow total concentration on the coordination of arms and legs. You may have to resort to float belts for the nonbuoyant.

Stay on the pool deck for increased visibility and call advice to individual students.

Equipment

- Masks and snorkels
- Float belts for the nonbuoyant

Instructions to Class

- ''When your wave is called, float, kick, and pull in correct coordination. Do not try to make any forward progress.''
- ''Breathe through your snorkel.''
- ''The next wave may pass through; you do not have to stay ahead of them.''

- ''Continue until you reach the other side or until I stop you.''
- ''Ones ready? Commence!''

Student Options

- ''Pass through the line ahead if they are not moving.''
- ''Move ahead of a slower student before starting.''

Student Keys to Success

- Good, clear demonstration
- Concentration on slow motion
- Good mental picture of the correct stroke

Student Success Goal

- 40 fully coordinated strokes

To Reduce Difficulty

- Decrease the number of strokes required.
- Talk the student through the stroke: ''Pull, heels up and hooked. . . . Kick the arms forward. . . . Glide.''

To Increase Difficulty

- Remove the mask and snorkel (but allow goggles), making student breathe during glide.

4. Breaststroke for Distance

[Corresponds to *Swimming*, Step 18, Drill 9]

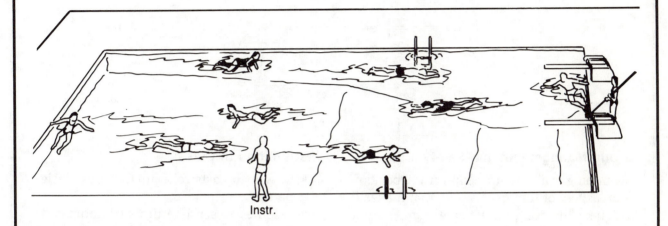

Instr.

Group Management and Safety Tips

For safety, have the students swim single file, far enough apart so there are not more than three or four in deep water at one time. Station the lifeguard at the deep end of the pool.

Explain the traffic pattern for 4 pool lengths as follows: "Start from the corner of the pool at the shallow end. Swim slightly diagonally, so you reach the deep end about 15 feet from the side edge. Grasp the end edge, tuck your knees, and pivot. Push off the wall at an angle so you get to the shallow end at the middle of the end wall. Turn again and push off at an angle that takes you to the deep end about 15 feet from the far pool side wall. To complete your zig zag course, push off and aim for the shallow corner opposite the starting corner." This traffic pattern keeps students from bumping into each other in midpool (maybe).

Equipment

- Goggles for those who wish
- Rescue equipment (particularly with this drill because a lot of students will be in deep water at the same time)

Instructions to Class

- "Wait for me to start you, then swim 4 lengths of breaststroke in the traffic pattern designated."
- "Swim slowly, take long glides, and relax."
- "Watch for other swimmers when you push off from the wall."

Student Options

- "Make a swimming turn, instead of pushing off from the wall."
- "Goggles are recommended for distance swimming."

Student Keys to Success

- Relaxation
- Smooth stroke
- Long glide

Student Success Goal

- An easy 100 yards

To Reduce Difficulty

- Shorten the distance required.
- Allow masks and snorkels.
- Swim beside the timid student.

To Increase Difficulty

- Increase the distance to 6 or 8 lengths. (Put competitive swimming lane lines in the pool. For 12 or less students, put 2 in a lane [6-lane pool] and have them swim side by side. For more than 12 [6-lane pool], put 3 or 4 in a lane and have them swim circles.)

5. Breaststroke Adaptation
[Corresponds to *Swimming*, Step 18, Drill 10]

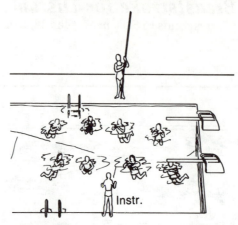

Group Management and Safety Tips

Swimming in a head-up, semi-vertical position is an aspect of the breaststroke that makes it unique. This drill *could* be taught in water of standing depth, but there is a danger of kicking the bottom. It *should* be taught in deep water, but only if you are confident in the ability of the students to handle it. If you are confident, you can save time by drilling the entire class at one time. If some students are hesitant about deep water, drill only a few at a time, or keep some in shallow water. Have the lifeguard watch.

Demonstrate the skill.

Have the students (according to your judgment) swim breaststroke into water deep enough for the skill and assume a head-up, semivertical position. Have them alternate kicking and stroking continually, without any glide at all. Tell them to stay low in the water; the lower they can stay (chin at water level), the easier it is.

Slow the stroke down to the bare minimum to stay afloat. Let them make some forward progress, but they should turn frequently to stay in a confined area. Talk to them, or make sure they talk to each other. (I try to tell them a long, drawn-out joke. It isn't funny, but it keeps their mind occupied.) Point out to them that this stroke adaptation is known as the "conversational" stroke. It allows them to swim and talk at the same time.

Equipment

- None

Instructions to Class

- "Swim breaststroke to the area designated."
- "Come to a semi-vertical position, heads up, alternate strokes and kicks with no glide."
- "Just swim in a small area until I tell you time is up."
- "Talk to each other."
- "We'll try to do 5 minutes. Swim to the side if you get tired."
- "Ready? Start."

Student Option

- Swim either in deep water or in the 5-foot area.

Student Keys to Success

- Stay low in the water
- Slow, easy strokes and kicks

Student Success Goal

- 5 minutes of continuous semivertical swimming

To Reduce Difficulty

- Have swimmer stay in shallow water.
- Reduce the time required.
- Allow reduced flotation in a flotation belt.
- Allow a back float position for short periods.

To Increase Difficulty

- Extend the time limit.
- Make your student laugh while he or she is trying to stay afloat.
- Insist that your student keeps the whole head out of water for short periods.

Step 19   Scissors Kick

The scissors kick is so easy to learn that even a beginner looks like an accomplished swimmer in a short time. No attempt should be made to rank a student on this skill. Simply correct the errors and the student will perform at the accomplished swimmer level.

Error Detection and Correction for the Scissors Kick

In the left-hand column below are listed several of the common errors beginners have in learning the scissors kick. The right-hand column offers some suggestions for correcting the errors.

ERROR

CORRECTION

1. Progress is diagonal, not straight ahead.

1. Body is not straight, caused by kicking toward the front. Have student step back farther with the lower leg until the thigh is in line with body.

2. Legs are apart laterally during kick.

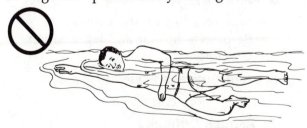

2. Have student, after stepping out forward and back, roll hips back so thighs are tight together. Explain that scissors don't cut unless the blades are tight together when closing, so no power would be derived from legs apart.

3. There is a short kick or no power.

3. After student steps out, feet should step out *even wider* as the thrust and squeeze begins.

Selected Scissors Kick Drills

1. Scissors Kick, Land Drill
[Corresponds to *Swimming*, Step 19, Drill 1]

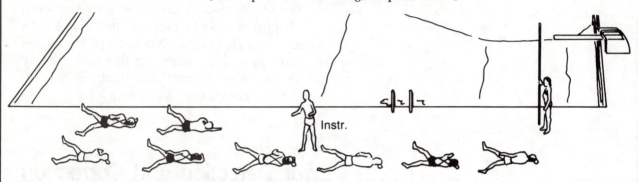

Group Management and Safety Tips

You need a deck area large enough for your class to lie down with legs widespread without kicking each other. If no such area is available, they can lie perpendicular to the edge of the pool with legs slightly over the water. Mats are best to lie on, but the bare deck may suffice. If the deck is abrasive, even a kickboard under the hip helps.

First, demonstrate the kick on the deck in slow motion. Have students lie on their sides, bodies straight, lower arm stretched forward under the head, and upper arm used to keep balance. Use a drill on command, starting with detailed commands, and progressing to key words or phrases.

Start to instruct your students like this: "Bring both knees up together until your hips are bent at 90 degrees. Keep your feet back in line with your body, not out in front of you." Now check and adjust the positions of each student.

Next say, "Hook the top ankle and point the toe of the lower foot. Step out forward with the top leg and step back with the lower leg until the lower thigh is straight with the body." Check each student and make corrections.

Then say, "Step out forward with the top leg and back with the lower leg as wide as you can, then thrust down and together like a pair of scissors. Point your toes at the end and don't let your feet pass. Glide."

Now on command, with key words, repeat the drill.

Equipment

- None

Instructions to Class

- "Stay together. Don't get ahead of me."
- "Knees up."
- "Hook and point."
- "Step out and back."
- "Drive. Glide."
- "Again. Up. Step out, around, and drive."

Student Option

- "Lie on either side."

Student Keys to Success

- Stay together on the commands
- Be precise in foot and leg positions
- Go slowly

Student Success Goal

- 10 or more correct kicks

To Reduce Difficulty

- Make the students as comfortable as possible.

To Increase Difficulty

- Require very precise movements.

2. Scissors Kick With Kickboard

[Corresponds to *Swimming*, Step 19, Drill 3]

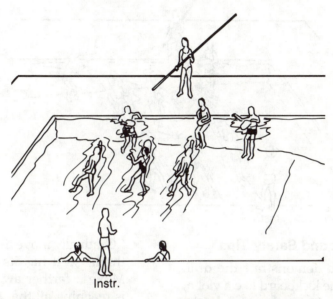

Instr.

Group Management and Safety Tips

Demonstrate this skill, showing the class two methods for holding the kickboard; let them choose whichever they like best. First show the board lengthwise on top of the top hip, held with the top arm over the board. Then show the ''violin'' position, with the board under the lower ear and the lower arm under the board, holding it like a violin.

Use a wave drill across the shallow area.

Equipment

- Kickboards

Instructions to Class

- ''When your number is called, hold the kickboard on your top hip or like a violin, as you prefer.''
- ''Use a wide, powerful scissors kick with a long glide across the pool.''

Student Options

- ''Choose which side to swim on.''
- ''Choose which method to use in holding the board.''

Student Keys to Success

- Slow, easy recovery
- Powerful thrust
- Long glide

Student Success Goal

- 1 pool width, or 45 feet

To Reduce Difficulty

- Allow 2 kickboards.
- Reduce the distance required.

To Increase Difficulty

- Remove the kickboard.
- Set the number of strokes allowed to reach the other side (or 45 feet).

3. Scissors Kick and Top Hand Push
[Corresponds to *Swimming*, Step 19, Drill 6]

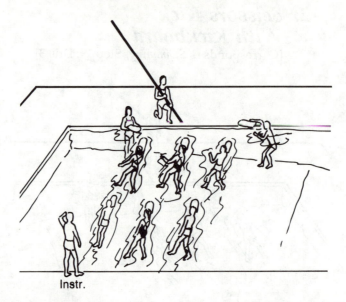

Instr.

Group Management and Safety Tips

Use a wave drill, and demonstrate the drill. Have students hold the kickboard like a violin, under the ear, with the forward arm under the board. They then start with the top hand resting on the front of the thigh. The hand stays at that spot on the thigh as the legs are recovered. During the drive of the legs, the top hand presses on the thigh as if to help it kick.

On the second or third kick, the top hand moves about 3 inches above the thigh but continues the same motion, pushing on the water near the thigh. Gradually the distance between hand and thigh is increased, until it is lifting nearly to the chin, and pushing hard on the water simultaneously with the leg thrust, coming to rest on the top of the leg at the end of the kick.

Equipment

- Kickboards

Instructions to Class

- ''When your number is called, scissors kick across the pool, your top hand helping the leg push against the water.''

- ''Gradually move the hand away from the thigh, so it has its own water to push. Move it farther away each time, until it is reaching all the way to the chin to get water to push against.''
- ''Let it rest on your leg during the long glide.''

Student Option

- ''Swim on either side.''

Student Key to Success

- Top hand gradually produces more of the propulsive force

Student Success Goal

- 40 kicks with hand push producing significant propulsion

To Reduce Difficulty

- Require a smaller number of strokes.
- Allow student to keep hand on thigh.

To Increase Difficulty

- Teach the correct arm motion for the sidestroke using top hand and kick only.
- Have students practice the kick and arm stroke on both sides.
- Have your students repeat the drill without the kickboard.

Step 20 Sidestroke Arm Motion

The sidestroke arm motion is a "partial" skill: It is only one part of the combination of skills that make up the sidestroke. Evaluation of the skill should come later, as a part of the whole stroke. It would be meaningless to evaluate a student on the basis of a partial skill.

Error Detection and Correction for the Sidestroke Arm Motion

The motion of each arm is distinct from the other, yet the two arms must be coordinated in their differences. Some of the errors that occur during the learning phase are listed on the left below. The right column suggests corrections for the errors.

ERROR

CORRECTION

1. Top hand pushes wide just under the surface.

1. At chin level, the top arm must be bent 90 degrees as the hands dig *down*. Hand and forearm must point directly down toward pool bottom and be about 6 inches in front of body for the push toward the feet.

2. Top wrist flexes, hand pushes water on the recovery.

2. Have student keep hand flat, keep wrist straight, and think about "slicing" the hand sideways through the water just under the surface. "Cut off the bottom of the ripples."

3. Forward arm digs deep, elbow straight.

3. Tell student, "Do not press on the water, but wrap your arm around an armful and gather it in."

4. Forward wrist flexes, pushes water on recovery

4. Have student, from the "palm-up-under-ear" position, shoot the fingertips forward as if to spear a fish.

Selected Sidestroke Arm Motion Drills

1. Sidestroke Forward Arm Pull, With Support

[Corresponds to *Swimming*, Step 20, Drill 1]

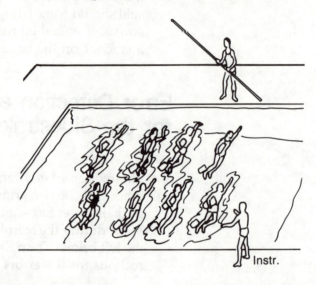

Instr.

Group Management and Safety Tips

Demonstrate the drill in very slow motion. Use the deep float leg support.

Because this is a floating drill with very little forward motion, a wave drill would take too long. Have the students count off by threes or fours and divide them into waves, but station the waves at intervals across the shallow area. Then all waves can begin at once in a mass drill. Insist that the students do not actually pull on the water but only move their arms slowly through the drill.

Once the motion has been established, you can run this drill again as a wave drill with forward motion.

Equipment

- Deep leg floats
- Kickboards

Instructions to Class

- "Lie on your side, top leg in the loop of the deep leg float, holding a kickboard under your top arm, pressed to your hip."

- "In *extreme* slow motion, go through the forward arm pull. Do not actually pull, but make the motion slowly."
- "Think! Concentrate on the elbow and hand positions."
- "Ready? Begin."

Student Option

- "Choose which side to use."

Student Keys to Success

- Extreme slow motion
- Concentration
- Repetition

Student Success Goal

- 40 correct arm pulls

To Reduce Difficulty

- Give individual attention.
- Reduce the number of strokes.

To Increase Difficulty

- After forward motion has been achieved, remove the kickboards.

2. Sidestroke Upper Arm Push, With Support
[Corresponds to *Swimming*, Step 20, Drill 2]

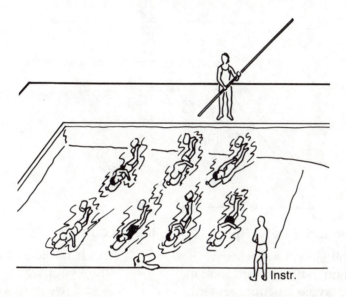

Group Management and Safety Tips

Demonstrate the drill in very slow motion.

A wave drill may be used for this drill, but the direction of motion for most will be a path that curves toward the student's back. Watch that none curve into the deep water. They can minimize the curve by keeping the thrust in close to the body. Curving can also be eliminated by using the feet as rudders; some students do this instinctively. Integrate the breathing into this drill.

Equipment

- Deep leg floats
- Kickboards

Instructions to Class

- "When your number is called, lie on your side with your top leg in the loop of the deep leg float and the kickboard in 'violin' position."
- "Slice the top hand up to your chin, dig in deep in front of your body, and push back toward the feet until your hand rests on your leg again."

- "Glide. If you curve toward your back, you are pushing too far away from your body."
- "Inhale on the recovery and exhale on the glide."

Student Option

- "Choose which side to use."

Student Keys to Success

- Push close to body with forearm and flat palm
- Bend elbow 90 degrees

Student Success Goal

- 40 upper arm thrusts with breathing and glide

To Reduce Difficulty

- Reduce the number of strokes required.
- Give individual attention.

To Increase Difficulty

- Have student drill on both sides.
- Remove the kickboards.

3. Coordinated Sidestroke Arm Pull, Feet Supported
[Corresponds to *Swimming*, Step 20, Drill 3]

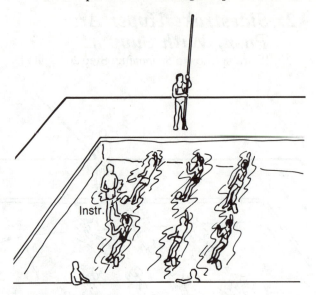

Group Management and Safety Tips

Demonstrate the drill slowly and clearly.

Use a wave drill, though the forward motion will not be rapid. To avoid discouragement, explain that not much forward progress is expected. Explain carefully the coordination between top and forward arms. Some students understand this better if it is likened to gathering an armful of water ahead, bringing it back to the chin, and letting the other hand pick it up there to push it on back to the feet, while the forward arm goes back for more.

Nonbuoyant students may require float belts for this drill.

Equipment

- Flotation belts, possibly
- Deep leg floats

Instructions to Class

- "Attach the leg float to your top leg."
- "When your wave is called, push off the side and use both arms in the sidestroke across the shallow area. Start very slowly to get the coordination, then speed up a little, but don't forget to take a long glide."
- "Inhale with the pull of the forward arm and exhale on the glide."

Student Option

- "You may swim on either side."

Student Keys to Success

- Concentration
- Slow motion at start

Student Success Goal

- 1 pool width, or 45 feet

To Reduce Difficulty

- Give individual attention.
- Reduce the distance required.

To Increase Difficulty

- Remove the leg support.
- Have student try both sides.
- Have student measure distance per stroke.

Step 21 Sidestroke

Even within a single class, the abilities of students differ considerably. It is helpful for you, the instructor, to be able to rank the students according to the quality of their skills. The table below can help in the evaluation and ranking of students into categories of beginner, novice, and accomplished by using four components of the sidestroke.

Sidestroke Rating

CHECKPOINT	BEGINNING LEVEL	NOVICE LEVEL	ACCOMPLISHED LEVEL
Arm Stroke **Forward Arm**	• Presses down • Elbow straight • Pushes water on recovery • Palm stays down	• Pulls past shoulder • Elbow bent 120 degrees • Elbow stays out • Palm up under ear	• Elbow bent 90 degrees • Pulls to chin • Elbow in • Palm up • Fingers lead recovery
Arm Stroke **Top Arm**	• Pulls wide • Elbow straight • Shallow • Pushes water on recovery	• Closer to body • Elbow bent • Deeper • Hand slices up • Overreaches	• Close to body • Elbow bent 90 degrees • Deep • Hand slices up • Digs in at chin
Kick	• Recover apart • Narrow • Does not step back • Lateral separation • Does not work ankles • Feet do not close	• Recover together • Wider • Does not step back • No separation • Ankles flex • Feet pass	• Recover together • Very wide • Steps way back • Thighs tight • Ankles flex • Feet do not pass
Body Position	• Head up • Bobbing • No glide • Body tense, bent	• Ear under • Level ride • Short glide • Body relaxed	• Ear under • Level ride • Long glide • Streamlined

Error Detection and Correction for the Sidestroke

Certain errors typically appear in this stroke, as in others. The table below lists errors in the left column and corrections for those errors in the right column.

ERROR	CORRECTION
1. Student does not swim straight, but moves off line toward back.	1. Caused by curved back and bent hips. Have student straighten body for kick and glide by stepping back much farther with bottom foot and consciously stretching for glide.
2. Feet pass each other at end of kick, causing drag and shorter glide.	2. Have student turn toes inward during kick so feet cross and stop when they meet. Student should stretch for streamlined glide.

Selected Sidestroke Drills

1. Forward Arm and Kick, Land Drill
[New drill]

Group Management and Safety Tips

If the pool coping permits, place your students around the edge of the pool on the deck. Have each lie down on the side, perpendicular to the edge, with head and shoulder over the water. The arm should hang down into the water. You may have to pad the edge or have them lie on kickboards if the gutter or coping interferes.

Use a drill on command, keeping everyone together through the drill. Start each in glide position, forward arm extended straight out over the water. Command, ''Pull with bent arm until hand and arm are flat against the pool wall. At the same time recover the legs together for the scissors kick.'' Hold them in this position until you can check all students.

Then command, ''Slide the hand up the wall under your ear, palm up, as the legs step out and back.'' Hold that position and check again.

Then command, ''Drive with the legs as the arm extends to glide position.''

Equipment

- Mats or something to alleviate the effects of lying on the coping or gutter

Instructions to Class

- ''Continue on command.''
- ''Pull, knees up.''
- ''Step out, hand to ear.''
- ''Kick, reach forward.''

Student Option

- ''Lie on either side.''

Student Keys to Success

- Move simultaneously with rest of class on command
- Learn coordination
- Repetition

Student Success Goal

- 10 or more strokes in correct coordination

To Reduce Difficulty

- Shorten the drill.
- Give individual attention.

To Increase Difficulty

- Require more strokes.

2. Forward Arm–Kick Coordination With Kickboard

[Corresponds to *Swimming*, Step 21, Drill 2]

Instr.

Group Management and Safety Tips

Demonstrate this drill.

Use a wave drill across the shallow area. Start your students moving in very slow motion until their coordination is good. Then speed up, but pause before the thrust to check their positions for a few strokes. Then eliminate the pause, have them perform the pull and kick alternately, but insist on a long glide.

Equipment

- Kickboards

Instructions to Class

- "When your number is called, push off the wall on your side, holding a kickboard under your top arm against your hip."
- "Start the arm pull; kick slowly until you get the timing, then pause before the kick for a few strokes."
- "When everything is timed properly, pull and kick smoothly, but take a l-o-n-g glide."
- "Stop at the other side."

Student Option

- "Swim on either side."

Student Keys to Success

- Easy, alternating kicks and pulls
- Long glides

Student Success Goal

- 40 or more strokes with correct coordination

To Reduce Difficulty

- Reduce the number of strokes required.

To Increase Difficulty

- Remove the kickboard.
- Drill student on both sides.
- Measure distance per stroke.

3. *Deep-Water Sidestroke*
[Corresponds to *Swimming*, Step 21, Drill 5]

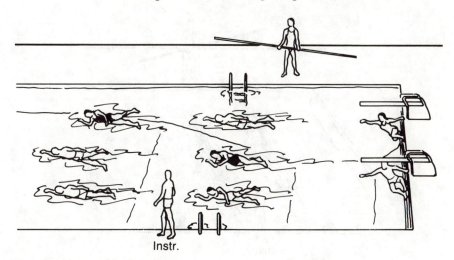

Instr.

Group Management and Safety Tips

Demonstrate the sidestroke with emphasis on holding the glide as long as possible. Remind the students that they can simply roll onto the back for safety if they wish. Have the lifeguard standing by.

Have the students count off by a number that will make waves of three each. Start from the deep end of the pool in waves of three. Allow a push-off from the end, and have the students count the number of strokes it takes to reach the shallow end of the pool.

Equipment

- None

Instructions to Class

- "When your number is called, push off from the end of the pool on your side."
- "Swim sidestroke to the shallow end. Stroke as powerfully as you can."
- "Streamline and ride each glide for distance."
- "Count the number of strokes you take to reach the end. Your goal is 12 strokes or less" [or the pool length in feet divided by 6].

Student Option

- "Swim on either side."

Student Keys to Success

- Take and hold large breaths
- Kick with power
- Streamline for the glide

Student Success Goal

- 6 feet or more on each stroke

To Reduce Difficulty

- Reduce the distance per stroke expected.

To Increase Difficulty

- Have student match the performance on the other side.
- Increase the expected distance per stroke.

4. *Lifesaving Sidestroke*
[Corresponds to *Swimming*, Step 21, Drill 8]

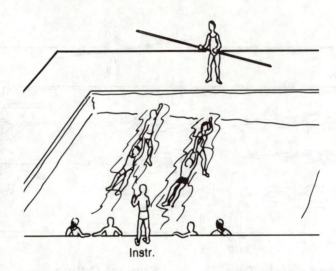

Instr.

Group Management and Safety Tips

Demonstrate swimming sidestroke with the forward arm and kick only, with the other arm carrying a 10-pound rubber-covered diving brick on your top hip. Also demonstrate towing a victim. Have a student float on the back with arms overhead. Grasp the student's hand and tow the "victim" across the pool.

Using a wave drill, have your students carry bricks across *and back* so the next wave can have the bricks. If you do not have bricks, use the tow instead. Let the students tow each other across the pool, switch "victim" and "rescuer" for the return trip.

Equipment

- 10-pound rubber-covered diving bricks (3 or more would be ideal, but none are necessary)

Instructions to Class

- "On command, swim across and back with the brick on your hip" or
- "Tow your buddy across the pool. Then you be the victim on the way back."
- "Do not try to glide—just kick and pull alternately."

Student Options

- "Carry the brick" (if available) or "tow a victim."
- "Swim on either side."

Student Keys to Success

- Powerful kick
- Continuous stroke and kick with no glide

Student Success Goals

- Carry a 10-pound brick either across the pool or 45 feet (the return trip exceeds the goal), or tow a victim across the pool.

To Reduce Difficulty

- Assign towing victim instead of carrying brick.
- Use no weight or victim, but have student simply hold the top hand up out of the water.

To Increase Difficulty

- Have swimmer carry a brick for a length instead of a width.
- Have students race across with bricks or relay race across and back towing victims.
- Have student carry 2 bricks across.

Step 22   Kneeling Dive

The kneeling dive is the first step in a progression to the standing front dive. Some students do the kneeling dive better than others, but it would not be useful to rank students as beginners, novice, or accomplished at such an elementary skill.

Error Detection and Correction for the Kneeling Dive

Errors are made even in this beginning step for diving. Some of the most common ones are mentioned in the left-hand column below. Suggested corrections appear in the right-hand column.

ERROR

CORRECTION

1. Forward leg strikes edge of pool.

1. Have student hook toes of the forward foot firmly over the edge of the pool. The leg can now strike only if the toes slip off the edge.

2. Rear leg strikes edge of pool.

2. Rear leg must be held straight and lifted from the hip as a unit.

3. Student strikes bottom of pool.

3. EXTREMELY DANGEROUS!! This error is usually the fault of the instructor and can be fatal. **NEVER** have anyone try this dive into less than 5 feet of water, from water level, or into less than 10 feet of water from a height greater than 1 foot. Be sure the student has been properly prepared by the preceding progressive steps.

4. Student somersaults.

4. Get into the water in front and slightly to the side of the student. Place a hand under student's hand and guide the student's hand upward on submersion. Student must stretch out and look up.

Selected Kneeling Dive Drills

1. *Underwater Glide*

[Corresponds to *Swimming*, Step 22, Drill 1]

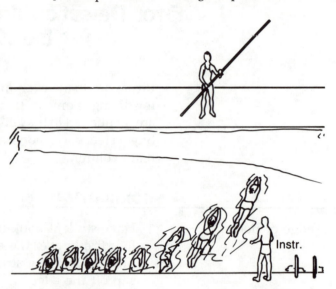

Group Management and Safety Tips

Demonstrate the drill.

Use a stagger drill. Have the students line up, back to the wall in water 4 1/2-5 feet deep. Have each place one foot against the pool wall and both arms over the ears. Then, one at a time on command, they should place the face in the water, aim slightly downhill, and push off.

Equipment

- None (do not permit goggles, because they would come off or would require wrong head position to keep them on)

Instructions to Class

- ''Back to the wall, one foot up. Arms over your ears, hook your thumbs and squeeze.''
- ''Listen for me to start you one at a time.''
- ''Push off, dig in as I showed you, and glide to the surface.''
- ''Ready? Go!''
- ''Next. Next. . . .''

Student Option

- None

Student Keys to Success

- Proper downward angle
- Long, easy glide

Student Success Goal

- 10 easy underwater glides

To Reduce Difficulty

- Assign a ''porpoise'' dive, jumping up from the bottom of the pool.
- Take student's hands and guide student through the glide.

To Increase Difficulty

- Require gliding for distance.

2. *Glide Through the Hoop*
[Corresponds to *Swimming*, Step 22, Drill 2]

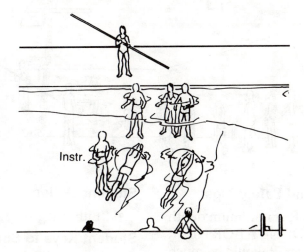

Group Management and Safety Tips

Demonstrate the drill.

Use 1, 2, or 3 hoops. If 1 hoop is used, line the students up along the wall and, after each student goes, move the hoop over in front of the next student. If 2 or 3 hoops are used, have the students move over in front of the hoops after each group of two or three students goes.

Students should place arms over ears and tuck both feet, floating in tucked position as they put both feet against the wall to push off.

Equipment

- Weighted hula hoops

Instructions to Class

- "Each one (or two or three) go on command."
- "Put your face in, tuck both legs tight, and push off through the hoop."

Student Option

- "Push off with one foot, if desired."

Student Keys to Success

- Good, solid push
- Long, streamlined glide

Student Success Goal

- 10 successful passes through the hoop

To Reduce Difficulty

- Cheat by moving hoop in front of erring student.
- Bring the hoop closer.

To Increase Difficulty

- Move the hoop farther away.
- Move the hoop to the side after student has pushed off, to see if student can change direction en route.

3. Kneeling Dive
[Corresponds to *Swimming*, Step 22, Drill 3]

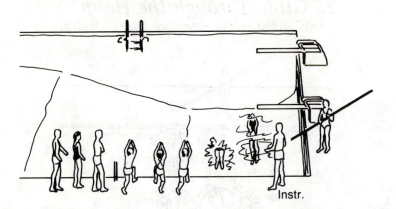

Instr.

Group Management and Safety Tips

You may use water of 5-foot minimum depth for a kneeling dive—IF DONE AT OR NEAR WATER LEVEL. However, it would be much safer to do all dives from whatever height in water of 10-foot depth.

Demonstrate this drill.

Have students kneel side by side on one knee along the edge of the pool over water of 10-foot depth. Have the lifeguard standing by. Use a stagger drill, each student starting on your command.

Equipment

- None (no goggles)

Instructions to Class

- ''Go one at a time on my command.''
- ''Toes firmly hooked over the edge, arms over your ears, thumbs hooked, squeeze.''
- ''Aim out and down.''
- ''Don't forget to lift that rear leg so it doesn't hit the edge.''
- ''Ready? Agatha, go!''
- ''Next. Next. . . .''

Student Option

- ''Either leg may be forward.''

Student Keys to Success

- Proper head and arm position
- Good toehold
- Lift rear leg

Student Success Goal

- 10 kneeling dives in good form

To Reduce Difficulty

- Be in water, catch student's hand immediately after entry, and guide student through pull-out and glide.

To Increase Difficulty

- Have student bring kneeling knee up off the deck into a ''track start'' position before diving.

Step 23   One-Foot Dive

CAUTION! THIS DIVE REQUIRES A WATER DEPTH OF AT LEAST 10 FEET. The one-foot dive is an interim dive in a progression toward the standing front dive. Nevertheless, it is sophisticated enough to stand on its own as a complete skill.

Students perform it with varying degrees of skill, and an experienced instructor can rank its performance by means of the chart below. It is here considered as a single entity, and no attempt has been made to rank individual components.

One-Foot Dive Rating

BEGINNING LEVEL	NOVICE LEVEL	ACCOMPLISHED LEVEL
• Hits flat	• Enters at 45 degrees	• Vertical entry
• Rear leg low	• Rear leg at 45 degrees	• Rear leg vertical
• Front knee collapses	• Front knee locked	• Feet together
• Rear leg hits edge	• Rear knee bent	• Toes pointed
• Somersaults	• Glides out 20 feet	• Surfaces at entry point
• Big splash	• Some splash	• Small splash

Error Detection and Correction for the One-Foot Dive

Errors in diving are usually more evident than errors in swimming. They take place above the water where they can be seen, and the result of an error is more spectacular—sometimes more painful. Some common errors are listed below with suggestions on how to correct them.

ERROR

CORRECTION

1. Forehead strikes water painfully.

1. Results from lifting chin and lowering arms. Have student keep arms tight over ears.

2. Top of head strikes water painfully.

2. Chin is in proper position, but arms are apart. Have student hook thumbs and keep arms and hands in front of head, over ears.

3. Diver lands on back.

3. Tell student, "*Lift* rear leg; don't kick it up. Aim a little farther out from edge. Keep back straight; bend only at hips. Keep legs straight; do not tuck. Lift head up a little."

Selected One-Foot Diving Drills

1. Transition From Kneeling Dive
[Corresponds to *Swimming*, Step 23, Drill 1]

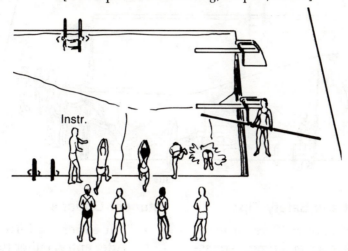

Instr.

Group Management and Safety Tips

CAUTION! All the following drills require 10 feet or more of water depth.

Demonstrate the dive several times, pointing out different aspects each time.

Use a stagger drill, with each student going individually on command, because it is impossible to see errors of more than one student at a time in the brief period allowed by a dive. They may go in rather rapid succession, however, to save time.

Line up your students along the deep-water edge of the pool in the kneeling position on one knee. Space them about 6 feet apart for safety. Caution them not to turn to the side after entry, but to come straight up or straight out.

Equipment

- None

Instructions to Class

- "Go one at a time on my command."
- "Keep your arms over your ears."
- "Raise your knee off the deck 6 or 8 inches to the 'track start' position. Aim a little closer to the wall, and dig in a little deeper."
- "Lift your rear leg high."
- "Ready? Christie, go!"
- "Next. Next. . . ."

Student Option

- "After entry, tuck, turn, and come to the surface, or glide out as before."

Student Keys to Success

- Once started do not hesitate
- Dig deep
- Raise the rear leg

Student Success Goal

- 5 "track start" dives in good form; in each one the leg on the kneeling side is lifted a little higher

To Reduce Difficulty

- Pay careful attention to beginning positions.
- Reinforce the mental image of the dive in the mind of the diver.

To Increase Difficulty

- Insist on straighter legs, more pointed toes, and more nearly vertical entry.

2. Correct One-Foot Dive

[Corresponds to *Swimming*, Step 23, Drill 2]

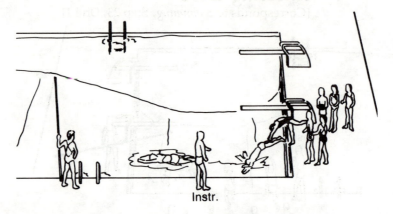

Instr.

Group Management and Safety Tips

Safety requires a water depth of 10 feet or more.

Demonstrate the dive several times, stressing the locked forward knee and the rear leg lift.

Use a stagger drill or a wave drill, but caution students on which way to turn after submersion.

Equipment

- None

Instructions to Class

- "Stand straight."
- "Hook the toes of one foot over the edge and move the other foot straight back about 2 feet."
- "Lock the knee of the forward foot. It is very important that it does not bend during the dive. If it bends, the rear leg could hit the deck, and I'm short of Band-aids."
- "Bend at the waist, arms over your ears, thumbs hooked."
- "On command, transfer all the weight onto your straight forward leg, tip forward, and lift your rear leg (not your foot) high up over your head as you enter the water."
- "Aim for a spot about 2 feet from the edge. Keep it in close."
- "Ready? Go!"

Student Options

- "Put either leg forward."
- "After entry, either tuck and turn or glide straight out."

Student Keys to Success

- Forward knee locked
- Both legs stretched straight
- Vertical entry

Student Success Goal

- 10 good one-foot dives.

To Reduce Difficulty

- Give an adequate demonstration.
- Pay attention to details of student's starting position.
- Establish for student a firm mental image of the dive.

To Increase Difficulty

- Make greater insistence on exact form, no splashing, and vertical entry.

3. Low Board Dive
[Corresponds to *Swimming*, Step 23, Drill 3]

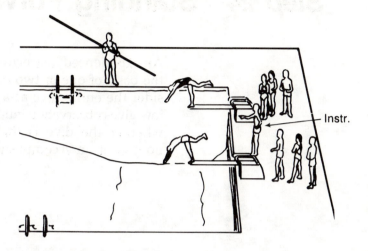

Group Management and Safety Tips

Demonstrate the skill. This is an individual skill. It must be performed by one student at a time. If two 1-meter boards are available, though, you may be able to drill two students at one time.

Have your student take the same stance on the board as previously at poolside, but aim a little farther out (about 3-4 feet out). Tell him or her not to raise the rear leg vigorously. Your student should raise the chin until he or she is looking at the water.

Your student should take care—the extra height makes it easier to flop over onto the back. Also, do not allow him or her to bounce the board up and down when diving.

Equipment

- One or two 1-meter diving boards

Instructions to Class

- "Move slowly out to the end of the board."
- "Hook the toes of one foot over the end."
- "Arms over your ears, and one foot back."
- "Bend at the waist and aim about 3 feet out. Look down between your arms at the water, and keep your head there."
- "Do the same dive as from the deck, but don't lift the rear leg as high."
- "Okay, go ahead. It's only water down there."

Student Option

- "Start with either leg forward."

Student Keys to Success

- No change of mind once started
- Have faith, summon courage, and dive with confidence

Student Success Goal

- 5 one-foot dives from a 1-meter board in good form and with confidence

To Reduce Difficulty

- Offer lots of sympathy and reassurance.
- Provide plenty of demonstrations until student thinks it looks easy. Have reluctant students go last.

To Increase Difficulty

- Do not increase the difficulty.

Step 24   Standing Forward Dive

An experienced instructor can rate a diver on the basis of one or two dives, but must consider the entire dive as a unit. The table below gives observation guidelines to determine whether the dive is that of a beginner, a novice, or an accomplished diver.

Standing Front Dive Rating

BEGINNING LEVEL	NOVICE LEVEL	ACCOMPLISHED LEVEL
• Stands still • No arm circle • No jump • No height • Legs apart • Knees bent • Toes relaxed • Not vertical • Big splash	• Bounces slightly • Arm swing is back and forward • Small jump • Some height • Legs together • Knees bent • Toes not pointed • Nearly vertical • Some splash	• Bounces rhythmically • Circular arm swing • Jumps from toes • Good height • Legs stretched • Knees straight • Toes stretched • Body stretched • Vertical entry • Very little splash

Error Detection and Correction for the Standing Front Dive

Some spectacular errors occur when people dive. Error prevention is important. It is accomplished by double-checking preparations, but there are always some errors to correct after the dive. The table below lists some common errors and suggests solutions for them.

ERROR 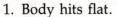   **CORRECTION**

1. Body hits flat.

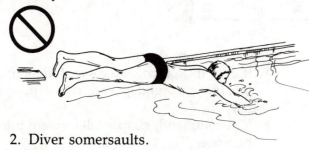

1. Have student keep chin down. When jumping, student should channel upward lift into hips so they rise behind body into semi-jackknife position. Divers should keep a mental image of jumping into a handstand on the water in front of them.

2. Diver somersaults.

2. Tell student to aim out farther; raise chin and look at water; keep body and legs straight; and bend only at waist. After bending, straighten out sooner for entry.

3. Diver falls in relaxed.

3. DIVER MUST NOT CHANGE MIND ONCE STARTING!

4. Diver is afraid.

4. Diver should have some faith in you, the instructor. After all it's only water down there. The very worst that could happen is a small temporary stinging. Tell student, "Remember, any 3-year-old can do it—with 5 years of practice."

Selected Standing Front Dive Drills

1. Standing, Two-Footed Fall-In Dive
[Corresponds to *Swimming*, Step 24, Drill 1]

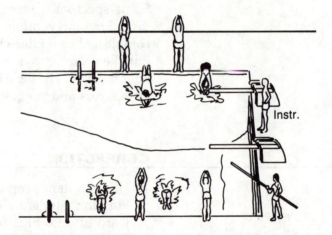

Instr.

Group Management and Safety Tips

This dive is very simple and can be done as a wave drill. The entire class can be lined up along the edge of the pool if you have room, but only every third or fourth student dives in a wave. This gives enough space between divers for safety.

This dive requires a *water depth of 10 feet or more* for safety. Be sure each wave of divers is completely clear of the area before the next wave dives. You may let students dive from both sides, if the pool width is at least 45 feet.

Demonstrate the dive several times.

Equipment

- None

Instructions to Class

- ''Stand ready at the edge but do not dive until your number is called.''
- ''Hook the toes of both feet over the edge.''
- ''Arms over your ears, thumbs hooked.''
- ''Bend forward at your waist until your hands point about 3 feet out from the edge.''
- ''Lock your knees straight and do not let them bend at any time in the dive.''

- ''Go straight down.''
- ''Either tuck, turn, and come straight up; or pull out, glide, and come up in midpool.''
- ''On command, simply fall forward into the water.''
- ''Ready ones? Go!''

Student Option

- ''After entry, either tuck, turn around, and surface; or arch, aim up, and glide to the surface.''

Student Keys to Success

- Keep knees straight
- Go straight down

Student Success Goal

- 3 fall-in dives with legs straight

To Reduce Difficulty

- Position the diver individually and encourage the fall.

To Increase Difficulty

- Start student higher, as from a 1-meter diving board.

2. Fall-In Dive With Spring
[Corresponds to *Swimming*, Step 24, Drill 3]

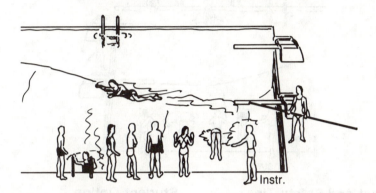

Instr.

Group Management and Safety Tips

The danger in this dive is in springing too early. If the diver springs before being off-balance, there is a danger of lifting straight up and coming down on the edge of the pool. For this reason, each student must do the dive with individual instruction. Students can be lined up on the pool edge but must wait for you to come and help the take-off.

This dive requires a *water depth of 10 feet or more*. Demonstrate this dive several times with emphasis on being totally off-balance before springing.

Equipment

• None

Instructions to Class

• "Do not dive until I get to you and start you."
• "Hook the toes of both feet over the edge."
• "Leave your arms hanging naturally at your side; or hold your hands at shoulder height, pointing upward to lead you in an up, over, and down path."
• "When I get to you, bend your knees slightly and keep your weight on the balls of your feet."
• "Then begin to fall forward."
• "When you are *definitely* past the point of no return, jump your hips up as your

head comes down. Go up 'over the fence' and come down on the other side."
• "Stretch your legs for the entry. Go straight down."

Student Options

• "Tuck your knees after entry and come directly to the surface, or pull out and glide to the top."
• "Start with your hands at your side and bring them forward as you fall, or start with your hands at shoulder height and extend them up, over, and down as you jump."

Student Keys to Success

• Be off-balance before jumping
• Make a vertical entry
• Stretch

Student Success Goal

• 3 fall-and-spring dives in good form

To Reduce Difficulty

• Give adequate preparation and demonstration.
• Impart a solid mental image of the dive.

To Increase Difficulty

• Take the dive to a higher starting point: Have student dive from a firmly anchored box or starting block in the deep end or from a 1-meter board.

3. Fully Coordinated Standing Front Dive
[Corresponds to *Swimming*, Step 24, Drill 5]

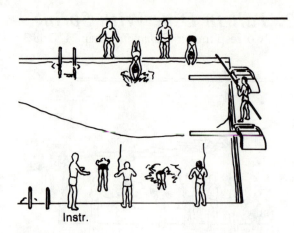

Instr.

Group Management and Safety Tips

Your students should perform this dive individually under direct supervision the first time it is done. After that, several may dive at one time so long as they have adequate spacing for safety. The students should be allowed to practice at their own speed for a time, while you wander around making suggestions. *The dive requires a water depth of 10 feet or more.*

Equipment

- None

Instructions to Class

- "Stand with your toes hooked over the edge."
- "Circle your arms and bend your knees at the same time."
- "Lean forward as your arms come forward past your legs; jump up, bend, and lift your legs up over your head."
- "Stretch for vertical entry, legs together, knees straight, and toes pointed."

Student Option

- "Tuck and come straight up, or pull out and glide."

Student Keys to Success

- Jump high
- Stay close to the edge
- Vertical entry
- Stretch
- No splash

Student Success Goal

- 10 fully coordinated standing front dives in good form

To Reduce Difficulty

- Give students adequate preparation.
- Give numerous demonstrations.

To Increase Difficulty

- Have student do the dive from the low diving board.

4. Hula Hoop-For-Height Dive

[Corresponds to *Swimming*, Step 24, Drill 6]

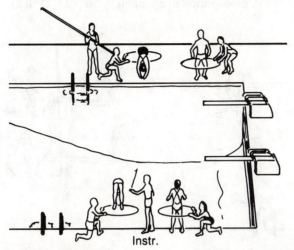

Instr.

Group Management and Safety Tips

This is a fun dive to induce the students to get more height in the standing front dive. It requires *10 feet or more* of water depth.

Have the class divide into buddy pairs. One will hold the hoop while the other dives. It would be ideal to have one hoop for each pair; otherwise, the buddies can take turns practicing diving while waiting for a hoop to become available.

Demonstrate the drill. Lay the hoop on the deck at water's edge. One student steps into the hoop and hooks toes over the edge. The second student kneels at the *side* of the first, picks up the hoop and raises it to the standing student's shins or knees. The hoop should be moved forward so there is plenty of clearance in front of the knees. When ready, the diver dives up out of the hoop and into the water. They should repeat this several times, raising the hoop each time. Try to get the diver to dive out of the hoop at hip height. The hoop holder must hold the hoop lightly, so it gives if the diver hits it.

Allow the students to work on their own while you make corrections.

Equipment

- As many hula hoops as are available

Instructions to Class

- "One buddy dives out of the hoop while the other holds it. The holder stands to the side to hold the hoop, so as not to get kicked by the diver's heels."
- "Start with the hoop at shin height and raise it each time to see how high your buddy can go."
- "Hold the hoop lightly and let it give if the diver hits it."
- "Change places."

Student Options

- "Go first or second."
- "Refuse any height."

Student Keys to Success

- Jump up, not out
- Keep knees straight
- Vertical entry

Student Success Goal

- 10 successful dives with the hoop at knee height or above

To Reduce Difficulty

- Have holder keep the hoop lower.
- Have diver practice first without the hoop.

To Increase Difficulty

- Have holder raise the hoop (stop when the diver screams "No, No!")
- Have student hold the hoop vertically, perpendicular to the edge in front of the diver, so the diver can, in effect, "roll over" the hoop into the water.

5. Fully Coordinated Standing Front Dive From Low Board

[Corresponds to *Swimming*, Step 24, Drill 8]

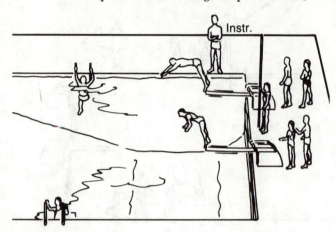

Group Management and Safety Tips

Safe diving practices dictate that 1-meter boards be mounted over water depths of *12 feet or more*. I would not suggest that anyone attempt to spring for height from a diving board in any lesser depth.

Students should not be required to do this dive. After four or five demonstration dives, the students may attempt this dive on their own from as many boards as are available. You should watch carefully, and make corrections and suggestions as necessary.

Equipment

- None

Instructions to Class

- "Stand at the end of the board and bounce *very* gently to sense the rhythm of the board's oscillation. Keep your weight on the balls of your feet."
- "Begin to circle your arms gently in rhythm with the board. Your arms should be moving forward past your thighs on each upward rise of the board."
- "Pick a number (3 or 4) to go on. Start to count each upward board motion; on your chosen number, spring upward just as you did from the hula hoop and dive. Pick a spot out a little farther (four or five feet) to hit."
- "Do not raise your feet vigorously—the board helps lift them."

- "Keep your head up."
- "The tendency is to flip over a little."

Student Option

- "You have the option of refusing to do this dive. A standing front dive from the edge is all that is required in this class."

Student Keys to Success

- Dive up, not down
- Keep the body fairly rigid; do not allow the body to relax in the air
- Achieve a vertical entry
- Stretch for a streamlined body

Student Success Goal

- 10 successful board dives with a streamlined, vertical entry

To Reduce Difficulty

- Give adequate preparation.
- Allow the student all the time desired, without pressure.
- Allow the student the option of not doing the dive.

To Increase Difficulty

- Start adding approach steps for a standard "running front dive." First, have student start with hurdle only; then, step, hurdle. Then, step, step, hurdle, followed by three steps and hurdle. Continue adding more steps as best suits the diver.

Evaluation Ideas

Teachers teach. Students learn. That's the way it is supposed to be. Determining whether the teacher has taught or the student has learned requires a process of evaluation. Changes that have occurred in the concepts, knowledge, or skill ability levels of the student must be evaluated by subjective or objective methods to determine how much teaching or learning has taken place.

Teaching Swimming: Steps to Success provides the tools an instructor needs to make valid decisions about students' progress. Only in this book will you find the unique Keys to Success and Success Goals which will help you evaluate students from beginner to accomplished performer.

As the student achieves performance objectives, the student's skill ability levels must be evaluated both quantitatively (how much, how far, how fast, how high) and qualitatively (how well, how smoothly, how confidently). The Success Goals in each step allow objective assessment of the quantitative aspects of each skill taught. The Keys to Success Checklists in *Swimming: Steps to Success* provide the means for a subjective evaluation of the qualitative aspects of each performance.

When both qualitative and quantitative evaluations are combined, students who are less skilled, less strong, smaller, or overweight nonetheless can experience success and achieve good grades. They are motivated toward practice, which also improves their performance scores. See Appendices C.1 and C.2 for a Sample Individual Program and a blank Individual Program evaluation sheet for your use in summarizing student progress.

You must make five evaluation decisions:

- How many skills or concepts can you or should you evaluate, considering the number of students and the time available?
- What specific quantitative or qualitative criteria do you wish to use to evaluate a specific skill?
- What relative weight do you wish to assign to any specific skill, considering its importance in the course?
- What type of grading system do you wish to use? For example, letter grades (A, B, C, D), satisfactory/unsatisfactory, number or point system (1, 2, 3, etc.), percentages (10%, 20%, 30%, etc.), or a system of achievement levels such as colors (red, white, blue), creatures (sharks, dolphins, minnows), or medallions (gold, silver, bronze).
- Who shall do the evaluating? You may designate certain quantitative evaluations to be made by the students' peers, up to a predetermined skill level, with all qualitative evaluations and all top grade determinations being made by the teacher.

I recommend that you hand out your evaluation program sheets at your first class meeting. These should encourage students to practice and improve, especially if they can assess each other by initialing observed scores on the quantitative evaluations (Success Goals) up to a "B" level (but they must demonstrate for the teacher [and get the teacher's initials] to receive an "A"). This avoids a one-chance pressure situation for the students, as they get used to performing in front of others, including the teacher, and gives them the entire unit's time to practice their skills. You may want to designate a few days near the end of your unit as the final testing days in which students can still improve their scores to qualify for the "A" or other top evaluation level. This avoids students' trying to increase their performance and technique scores beyond the deadline you set.

If you are working with very large classes spanning three or more grade levels, select only four to six objectives. Include quantitative objectives that permit self-testing. This testing can involve parents, brothers, sisters, or friends to verify that the goals up to a certain level of performance—for example, a "B" grade—have been reached by the student. The qualitative objectives should more likely involve peer evaluations with some teacher evaluation.

Objectives in a swimming course are usually skills that are important for safety, skills that lead students to important discoveries about their relationship to the water, or "whole stroke" proficiency. Qualitative objectives might be such things as technical expertise in the elementary backstroke; correct foot, leg, and ankle action in the crawl stroke kick; ability to turn over smoothly from front to back; or near-perfect form in a standing front dive. Some quantitative objectives would include 40 continuous scissors kicks in good form, 5 minutes of continuous back-floating with no aids, or swimming the crawl stroke 100 yards nonstop.

In some instances, a planned program of instruction may be adjusted for specific students who are lagging behind the class or are bored because they are so far ahead in skills. For instance, the person whose ankles are too stiff to produce propulsion in the crawl kick may be permitted to wear swim fins for all crawl stroke drills. New, simpler Success Goals may be formulated for the youngster in a class of adults or the student who has the use of only one leg. The swimmer who is ahead of the class in sidestroke might be required to do all the sidestroke drills on the side opposite the usual one. An advanced crawl stroke student might find a challenge in breathing on both sides (every third arm stroke).

If you are expecting cognitive as well as psychomotor improvement from your students, you may indicate at the beginning of the course that they will be expected to remember the concepts, coordinations, and physical laws that are embodied in the course and that they will be asked to indicate this knowledge retention by answering a few questions at the end of the course.

A sample written exam is offered below, from which you may select questions for your own:

_____

Name: _____

Class: _____ Date: _____

SWIMMING EXAM

Directions: Please write "True" or "False" in the space at the left side of the question number.

_____ 1. The human body is lighter than water, and all humans can float motionless.

_____ 2. Buoyancy is a function of lung capacity and fat tissue in relationship to muscle and bone structure.

_____ 3. Each person has an individual body makeup that determines what percentage of the body remains above water during floating.

_____ 4. Balance plays no part in determining the position of a floating person.

_____ 5. A relaxed body weighs less, so it floats better.

_____ 6. Holding your breath, arching your back, and holding still, you assume a face up position.

_____ 7. Bending forward at the hips assures a faceup floating position.

_____ 8. The natural floating position for most people is horizontal.

_____ 9. In a back float, your feet come closest to the surface if you extend your arms underwater as far beyond your head as you can.

_____ 10. The support kick resembles riding a bicycle.

_____ 11. The support kick and the back crawl kick are performed exactly the same way.

_____ 12. In the support kick, the soles of the feet press downward on the water.

_____ 13. The foot lifts water up and back in the back crawl kick.

_____ 14. When sculling, the hands move perpendicular to the direction of the force applied to the water.

_____ 15. Sculling provides forward motion but no support.

_____ 16. *Polish the wall* refers to a motion in the elementary backstroke arm stroke.

_____ 17. Thumbs should slide up along the sides in the elementary backstroke arm motion.

_____ 18. At the end of the recovery of the elementary backstroke arm motion, the thumbs should be on top of the shoulders.

_____ 19. The fingertips lead in the catch of the elementary backstroke arm motion.

_____ 20. The pull of the elementary backstroke begins about 6 inches below shoulder level.

_____ 21. Pressing down on the water during the backstroke pull keeps the body riding level.

_____ 22. A long glide should follow the backstroke arm pull.

_____ 23. Kicking during a backstroke pull destroys the rhythm of the pull.

_____ 24. Pulling with only one arm in the backstroke causes your body to turn toward the pulling arm.

_____ 25. Sculling with only one hand causes your body to turn away from the sculling hand.

_____ 26. A prone float is more pleasant because your face is always out of the water.

_____ 27. Bending forward at the waist and sliding your hands down your legs to the ankles is called the ''jackknife'' float.

_____ 28. A floating person holding the breath but otherwise completely relaxed always floats face down.

_____ 29. Some forward motion is necessary for the prone float..

_____ 30. The knees should be kept perfectly straight during the beginner kick.

_____ 31. Propulsion is derived from the backward push of the legs and feet in the beginner kick.

_____ 32. Support is derived from the downward push of the legs and feet in the beginner kick.

_____ 33. It is not possible to derive both support and propulsion from a kick.

_____ 34. The elbow bends during the beginner pull.

_____ 35. The elbow leads the hand on the recovery of the beginner pull.

_____ 36. One arm pulls while the other recovers in the beginner pull.

_____ 37. The major portion of the pull should be under the centerline of the body in the beginner pull.

_____ 38. The beginner pull ends at the waist.

_____ 39. Inhale through the mouth in all swimming strokes.

_____ 40. Exhaling partly through the nose is a good practice.

_____ 41. Humming while learning to breathe in swimming is considered poor practice.

_____ 42. When rolling from front to back, bend forward to assist the roll.

_____ 43. Tucking the legs helps greatly in making a turnover through the vertical position.

_____ 44. The side glide is a stunt with no utilitarian value.

_____ 45. Balance is maintained in the side glide by minor adjustments in the bend of the hips.

_____ 46. The elbow leads the hands in the recovery of the overhand arm stroke.

_____ 47. Fingertips should enter the water before the elbow on the overhand stroke.

_____ 48. *Over the barrel* refers to an old method of artifical respiration in our swimming class.

_____ 49. A very important part of the overhand recovery is keeping the elbow high during the recovery and on the entry.

_____ 50. The crawl stroke requires six kicks to each complete arm stroke; any other count is incorrect.

_____ 51. Swimmers must breathe to the right when doing the correct crawl stroke.

_____ 52. The shoulders should remain perfectly flat in the crawl stroke.

_____ 53. A good crawl stroke swimmer can breathe equally well on either side.

_____ 54. The crawl stroke is the fastest stroke known.

_____ 55. The crawl stroke uses energy more efficiently than any other stroke.

_____ 56. The stroke that *conserves* energy most efficiently is the elementary backstroke.

_____ 57. Arms and legs finish the power phase virtually at the same instant in the elementary backstroke.

_____ 58. The feet lead the knees outward prior to the power phase of the elementary backstroke kick.

_____ 59. The knees should be very close at all times during the elementary backstroke kick.

_____ 60. The breaststroke pull finishes at shoulder level.

_____ 61. The breaststroke kick and the elementary backstroke kick are virtually the same.

_____ 62. Arm-leg coordination is the same for the breaststroke and the elementary backstroke.

_____ 63. Breaststroke coordination should be pull-kick-glide.

_____ 64. The bottom leg steps forward in the standard scissors kick.

_____ 65. The top hand works in opposition to the forward arm in the sidestroke.

_____ 66. The top hand pushes simultaneously with the top leg in the sidestroke.

_____ 67. The sidestroke ends with a long glide.

_____ 68. The sidestroke is used for towing others in lifesaving.

_____ 69. A longer glide is used when towing a victim.

_____ 70. The sidestroke is one of the strokes used in competitive swimming.

_____ 71. A hula hoop is sometimes used in learning the kneeling dive.

_____ 72. A vertical entry is expected on a one-foot dive.

_____ 73. Maximum height is desirable on a standing front dive.

_____ 74. A hula hoop is useful in learning the standing front dive.

_____ 75. A minimum depth of 10 feet is required for both the one-foot dive and the standing front dive.

_____ 76. The amount of splash is an indication of the excellence of a dive.

_____ 77. A standing front dive should include a coordinated arm swing.

_____ 78. Diving has no place in a swimming course and should not be part of the course.

_____ 79. True/false tests are the pits.

_____ 80. More of these answers are true than false.

SWIMMING EXAM ANSWER KEY

1. False	21. False	41. False	61. True
2. True	22. True	42. False	62. False
3. True	23. False	43. True	63. True
4. False	24. False	44. False	64. False
5. False	25. True	45. True	65. True
6. True	26. False	46. True	66. True
7. False	27. False	47. True	67. True
8. False	28. True	48. False	68. True
9. True	29. False	49. True	69. False
10. True	30. False	50. False	70. False
11. False	31. True	51. False	71. True
12. True	32. True	52. False	72. True
13. True	33. False	53. True	73. True
14. True	34. True	54. True	74. True
15. False	35. False	55. True	75. True
16. False	36. False	56. True	76. True
17. True	37. True	57. True	77. True
18. True	38. False	58. True	78. Student choice
19. True	39. True	59. False	79. Student choice
20. False	40. True	60. True	80. True

Appendices

Appendix A
How to Use the Knowledge Structure Overview

A knowledge structure is an instructional tool—by completing one you make a very personal statement about what you know about a subject and how that knowledge guides your decisions in teaching and coaching. The knowledge structure for swimming outlined here has been designed for a teaching environment, with teaching progressions that emphasize technique and performance objectives in realistic settings. In a coaching environment, you would need to emphasize more physiological and conditioning factors, with training progressions that prepare athletes for competition.

The Knowledge Structure of Swimming shows the first page or an *overview* of a completed knowledge structure. The knowledge structure is divided into broad categories of information that are used for all of the participant and instructor guides in the Steps to Success Activity Series. Those categories are

- physiological training and conditioning,
- background knowledge,
- psychomotor skills and tactics, and
- psycho-social concepts.

Physiological training and conditioning has several subcategories, including warm-up and cool-down. Research in exercise physiology and the medical sciences has demonstrated the importance of warming up before and cooling down after physical activity. The participant and instructor guides present principles and exercises for effective warm-up and cool-down, which, because of time restrictions, are usually the only training activities done in the teaching environment. In a more intense coaching environment, additional categories should be added—training principles, injury prevention, training progressions, and nutrition. Notice that this swimming knowledge structure also includes cardiovascular conditioning.

The background-knowledge category outlines subcategories of essential background knowledge that all instructors should have mastery of when beginning a class. For swimming, background knowledge includes physical laws, such as buoyancy and propulsion.

Under psychomotor skills and tactics, all the individual skills in an activity are named. For swimming, these are shown as the vertical float, balance floats (back, front, side), sculling, backstroke, prone stroke, crawl stroke, breaststroke, sidestroke, and diving. These skills are also presented in a recommended order of presentation. In a completed knowledge structure, each skill is broken down into subskills, delineating selected technical, biomechanical, motor learning, and other teaching and coaching points that describe mature performance. These points can be found in the Keys to Success and the Keys to Success Checklists in the participant book.

The psycho-social category identifies selected concepts from the sport psychology and sociology literature that have been shown to contribute to learners' understanding of and success in the activity. These concepts are built into the key concepts and the activities for teaching. For swimming, the concept identified is fear reduction: perception, assurance, and attitude.

To be a successful teacher or coach, you must convert what you have learned as a student or done as a player or performer to knowledge that is conscious and appropriate for presentation to others. A knowledge structure is a tool designed to help you with this transition and to speed your *steps to success*. You should view a knowledge structure as the most basic level of teaching knowledge you possess for a sport or activity. For more information on how to develop your own knowledge structure, see the theory textbook that accompanies this series, *Instructional Design for Teaching Physical Activities*.

Appendix A
Knowledge Structure of Swimming (Overview)

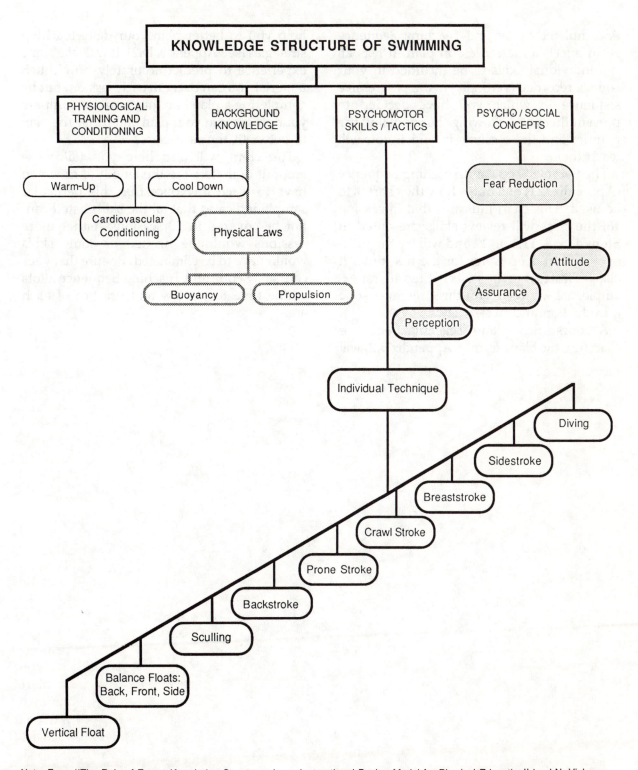

Note. From ''The Role of Expert Knowledge Structures in an Instructional Design Model for Physical Education'' by J.N. Vickers, 1983, *Journal of Teaching in Physical Education*, **2**(3), pp. 25, 27. Copyright 1983 by Joan N. Vickers. Adapted by permission. This Knowledge Structure of Swimming was designed specifically for the Steps to Success Activity Series by Joan N. Vickers, Judy P. Wright, and David G. Thomas.

Appendix B.1
How to Use the Scope and Teaching Sequence Form

A completed Scope and Teaching Sequence is, in effect, a master lesson plan. It lists all the individual skills to be included in your course, recorded (vertically) in the progressive sequence in which you have decided to present them and showing (horizontally) the manner and the sessions in which you will teach them.

The Sample Scope and Teaching Sequence (Appendix B.1) illustrates how the chart is to be used. This chart indicates that in session 16, the class will review skills presented in Steps 4, 6, 8, 11, and 12 and will try the turnover skill in deep water for the first time. It also indicates that the skills in Step 10, for example, are worked on for three sessions—one introduction and two reviews.

A course Scope and Teaching Sequence chart (use the blank form in Appendix B.2) will help you to better plan your daily teaching strategies (see Appendix D.2). It will take some experience to predict accurately how much material you can cover in each session, but by completing a plan like this, you can compare your progress to your plan and revise the plan to better fit the next class.

The chart will also help you tailor the amount of material to the length of time you have to teach it. Notice that this particular sample indicates that all the skills listed cannot be covered in 30 sessions—either more sessions would be needed or some skills would have to be eliminated. Be sure that your course's Scope and Teaching Sequence allots ample time for review and practice of each area.

Appendix B.1
Sample Scope and Teaching Sequence

N	New	R	Review	C	Continue	T	Test

NAME OF ACTIVITY: Swimming
LEVEL OF LEARNER: Beginning

Steps	Session Number	1	2	3	4	5	6	7	8	9	10	11	12	13	14	15	16	17	18	19	20	21	22	23	24	25	26	27	28
1	Buoyancy (deep water)	N																										R	
1	Buoyancy (shallow water)	C																											
2	Back float (shallow)	N	R	R		R	R																						
2	Back float (deep)		C																									R	T
3	Sculling (shallow)		N	R																									
3	Sculling (deep)		C																						R			R	T
4	El. backstroke arms (shallow)				N	R	R																			R			
5	Support kick back (shallow)				N	R	R																						
6	Back crawl kick (shallow)					N	R																						
4-6	Kick and pull back (shallow)						C	R																		R			
4-6	Kick and pull back (deep)							C	R	R							R								R			R	T
7	Prone float (shallow)								N																				
8	Beginner kick (shallow)								N	C	R	R																	
9	Beginner pull (shallow)									N	C		R	R															
10	Breathing, prone (shallow)											N	R	R															
11	Pull and breathe, prone (shallow)												N	C	R														
8-11	Kick, pull, breathe, prone (shallow)													N	R	R													
8-11	Kick, pull, breath, prone (deep)														C	R	R								R				
12	Turning over (shallow)															N	R												
12	Turning over (deep)																C	R							R			R	T
13	Side glide (shallow)																	N	C	R	R		R						
14	Overhand stroke (shallow)																		N	C	C	R	R	R			R		
15	Crawl stroke (shallow)																			N	C	C	R						
15	Crawl stroke (deep)																						C	C				R	T
16	El. backstroke (shallow)																								N	R			
16	El. backstroke (deep)																										C	R	T
17	Breaststroke pull (shallow)																												
18	Breaststroke (shallow)																												
18	Breaststroke (deep)																												
19	Scissors kick (shallow)																												
20	Sidestroke pull (shallow)																												
21	Sidestroke (shallow)																												
21	Sidestroke (deep)																												
22	Kneeling dive (5–10 ft. water)																												
23	One-foot dive (deep)																												
24	Standing forward dive (deep)																												

Appendix B.2

Scope and Teaching Sequence

| | New N | Review R | Continue C | Student Directed Practice P | | | NAME OF ACTIVITY _____ |
| | | | | | | | LEVEL OF LEARNER _____ |

Steps	Session Number	1	2	3	4	5	6	7	8	9	10	11	12	13	14	15	16	17	18	19	20	21	22	23	24	25	26	27	28	29	30
1																																
2																																
3																																
4																																
5																																
6																																
7																																
8																																
9																																
10																																
11																																
12																																
13																																
14																																
15																																
16																																
17																																
18																																
19																																
20																																
21																																
22																																
23																																
24																																
25																																

Note. From *Badminton: A Structures of Knowledge Approach* (pp. 60-61) by J.N. Vickers and D. Brecht, 1987, Calgary, AB: University Printing Services. Copyright 1987 by Joan N. Vickers. Adapted by permission.

Appendix C.1
How to Use the Individual Program Form

To complete an individual program for each student, you must first make five decisions about evaluation:

1. How many skills or concepts can you or should you evaluate, considering the number of students and the time available? The larger your classes and the shorter your class length, the fewer objectives you will be able to use.
2. What specific quantitative or qualitative criteria will you use to evaluate specific skills? See the Sample Individual Program (Appendix C.1) for ideas.
3. What relative weight is to be assigned to each specific skill, considering its importance in the course and the amount of practice time available?
4. What type of grading system do you wish to use? Will you use letters (A, B, C, D), satisfactory/unsatisfactory, a number or point system (1, 2, 3, etc.), or percentages (10%, 20%, 30%, etc.)? Or you may prefer a system of achievement levels, such as colors (red, white, blue), creatures (sharks, dolphins, minnows), or medallions (gold, silver, bronze).
5. Who will do the evaluating? You may want to delegate certain quantitative evaluations to be made by the students' peers up to a predetermined skill level (e.g., a "B" grade), with all qualitative evaluations and all top-grade determinations being made by you.

Once you have made these decisions, draw up an evaluation sheet (using Appendix C.2) that will fit the majority of your class members. Then decide whether you will establish a minimum level as a passing/failing point. Calculate the minimum passing score and the maximum attainable score, and divide the difference into as many grade categories as you wish. If you use an achievement-level system, assign a numerical value to each level for your calculations.

The blank Individual Program sheet, as shown in Appendix C.2, is intended not to be used verbatim (although you may do so if you wish), but rather to suggest ideas that you can use, adapt, and integrate with your own ideas to tailor your program to you and your students.

Make copies of your program evaluation system to hand out to each student at your first class meeting, and be prepared to make modifications for those who need special consideration. Such modifications could be changing the weight assigned to particular skills for certain students, or substituting some skills for others, or varying the criteria used for evaluating selected students. Thus, individual differences can be recognized within your class.

You, the instructor, have the freedom to make the decisions about evaluating your students. Be creative. The best teachers always are.

Appendix C.1

Sample Individual Program

INDIVIDUAL COURSE IN _____   GRADE/COURSE SECTION _____

STUDENT'S NAME _____   STUDENT ID # _____

SKILLS/CONCEPTS	TECHNIQUE AND PERFORMANCE OBJECTIVES	WT* ×	POINT PROGRESS** 1	2	3	4	= FINAL SCORE***
Back Float	*Technique:* Back fully arched, arms extended overhead. Breathes fully, easily. Relaxed. Scoops and recovers smoothly.	0.5					
Kick and Pull on Back	*Technique:* Recovers arms to top of shoulder. Reaches high and far for catch. Pulls full and level. Long glide. Ankles flex properly. Knees and feet stay under. Relaxed, rhythmical kick.	1.0					
	Performance: Moves well with moderate speed in deep water. Swims 45–150 ft.	1.0	45 ft	90–100 ft	100–125 ft	150+ ft	
Prone Kick, Pull, Breathe	*Technique:* Full reach forward. Catch with high elbow. Elbow bent 90°. Pulls long, one arm at a time. Kicks easily. Flexible ankles. Some knee bend. Breathes easily. One side only. Ear on water.	1.5					
	Performance: Moves smoothly with no distress. Swims 45–150 ft.	1.5	45 ft	60–90 ft	100–125 ft	150+ ft	
Turning Over	*Technique:* Does both rolls and through-vertical turnovers. Does both front-to-back and back-to-front rolls smoothly, head remains up. Tucked legs pass through smoothly on vertical turnovers.	1.0					
Crawl Stroke	*Technique:* Long reach, full pulls. Lifts shoulders for recovery. High elbows. Elbow leads hand on recovery. Fingertips enter before elbows. Steady, relaxed kick. 2, 4, or 6 beats. Breathes low on pull. Flows smoothly. Effortless.	1.75					
	Performance: Breathes every stroke. Swims with relative ease 45 ft to 100 yd.	1.5	45 ft	50 yd	75 yd	100 yd	

	Description	WT	25 yd	50 yd	75 yd	100+ yd
Elementary Backstroke	*Technique:* Smooth arm recovery; high catch; long, full pulls. Long glide. Relaxed. Feet hook as they drop back. Hooked feet turn out. Wide kick with inside of foot/ankle. Streamlined. Toes pointed. Kick, stroke finish together.	1.0				
	Performance: Each stroke covers 6 ft or more. Relaxed long glide of 25–100 yd.	1.0	25 yd	50 yd	75 yd	100+ yd
Breaststroke	*Technique:* Does not pull past shoulders. Hands dig in. Elbow 90°. Coordination is pull-kick-glide. Long glide. Breathes low. Breathes at end of pull. Legal kick. Knees narrow, feet hooked.	1.5				
	Performance: Smooth, at least 8–10 ft per stroke. Swims 25–100 yd.	1.5	25 yd	50 yd	75 yd	100+ yd
Sidestroke	*Technique:* Head down. Arms work in exact opposition. Top arm works exactly with leg. Kick. Top leg forward. Stays exactly on side. Strong kick, long glide, streamlined. Feet do not pass.	1.0				
	Performance: Smooth. Each stroke equals at least 6 ft. Swims 25–100 yd.	1.0	25 yd	50 yd	75 yd	100+ yd
One-Foot Dive	*Technique:* Forward knee locked. Rear legs straight. Toes hooked over edge. Lifts rear leg to vertical. Vertical entry. Body stretched. Feet together. Knees straight. Toes pointed. Very small splash.	1.0				
Standing Front Dive	*Technique:* Arms circle. Good height. Legs lift together. Toes pointed. Vertical entry. Body stretched, streamlined. Stays in close. Very little splash.	1.5				
	Performance: Achieves 4–10 *consecutive* dives (or 4 in 10 trials) displaying good technique.	1.0	4 4/10	6 6/10	8 8/10	10 10/10
Exam on Knowledge of Technique	Value = 25%					

*WT = Weighting of an objective's degree of difficulty.

**PROGRESS = Ongoing success, which may be expressed in terms of (a) accumulated points (1, 2, 3, 4); (b) grades (D, C, B, A); (c) symbols (merit, bronze, silver, gold); (d) unsatisfactory/satisfactory; and others as desired.

***FINAL SCORE equals WT times PROGRESS.

Appendix C.2

Individual Program

INDIVIDUAL COURSE IN _____

STUDENT'S NAME _____

GRADE/COURSE SECTION _____

STUDENT ID # _____

SKILLS/CONCEPTS	TECHNIQUE AND PERFORMANCE OBJECTIVES	WT* ×	POINT PROGRESS** =				FINAL SCORE****
			1	2	3	4	

Note. From "The Role of Expert Knowledge Structures in an Instructional Design Model for Physical Education" by J.N. Vickers, 1983, *Journal of Teaching in Physical Education*, **2**(3), p. 17. Copyright 1983 by Joan N. Vickers. Adapted by permission.

*WT = Weighting of an objective's degree of difficulty.

**PROGRESS = Ongoing success, which may be expressed in terms of (a) accumulated points (1, 2, 3, 4); (b) grades (D, C, B, A); (c) symbols (merit, bronze, silver, gold); (d) unsatisfactory/satisfactory; and others as desired.

***FINAL SCORE equals WT times PROGRESS.

Appendix D.1
How to Use the Lesson Plan Form

All teachers have learned in their training that lesson plans are vital to good teaching. This is a commonly accepted axiom, but there are many variations in the form that lesson plans can take.

An effective lesson plan sets forth the objectives to be attained or attempted during the session. If there is no objective, then there is no reason for teaching, and no basis for judging whether the teaching is effective.

Once you have named your objectives, list specific activities that will lead to attaining each. Every activity must be described in detail—what will take place and in what order, and how the class will be organized for the optimum learning situation. Record key words or phrases as focal points as well as, particularly in swimming, brief reminders of the applicable safety precautions.

Finally, set a time schedule that allocates a segment of the lesson for each activity to guide you in keeping to your plan. It is wise to also include in your lesson plan a list of all the teaching and safety equipment you will need, as a reminder to check for availability and location of the equipment before class.

An organized, professional approach to teaching requires preparing daily lesson plans. Each lesson plan provides you with an effective overview of your intended instruction and a means to evaluate it when class is over. Having lesson plans on file allows someone else to teach in your absence.

You may modify the blank Lesson Plan shown in Appendix D.2 to fit your own needs, just as I have modified it in the sample to include an equipment list.

Appendix D.1
Sample Lesson Plan

Lesson plan _____ 2 _____ of _____ 30 _____   Activity __ Beginner Swimming __

Class __ 1:30–2:45 Tu–Th (10 students) __

Objectives:	Equipment needed:
1. Student warms up.	3 buoyancy belts
2. Student reviews, practices buoyancy (deep).	reaching pole for lifeguard
3. Student is briefly introduced to back float.	whistle
4. Student is briefly introduced to sculling.	3-4 noseclips
5. Student is introduced to bobbing as taper.	

Skill or concept	Learning activity	Teaching points	Time (min)

1. Warm-up	• On mats, bleacher area.
	  Quick breathing and breath-holding
	  Head tilt, roll
	  Arm circles
	  Torso bends
	  Ankle flexes
		• Reinforce importance
		• Have students start on arrival hereafter
			5

2. Buoyancy review (deep)	• Demonstrate
	  Warn to wait for me
	  One at a time
	  At deep corner
		• Lifeguard alert!
		  Big breath
		  Relax
			20

3. Introduce back float (shallow)	• Around shallow corner demonstrate
	  Fingertips (2) on wall
	  Individual help first time, then pair off with buddy
		• Have students *walk* back to shallow end
		• Leave heels on floor of pool!
		• Show how to help as buddy
			15

| 4. Introduce sculling (shallow) | • Demonstrate Explain mechanics, physics
Mass drill: standing
Mass drill: "Polish the Wall" in front of them (around shallow corner)
Wave drill (3-3-4) in back float from side | • *Why* it is important
• "Polish the Wall" | 15 |
| 5. Taper with bobbing | • Spread out in shallow area
• Demonstrate Bobbing
Students try it on their own | • Inhale: mouth only
• Exhale: "hum it out" | 5 |

Appendix D.2
Lesson Plan

LESSON PLAN _____ OF _____   OBJECTIVES:

ACTIVITY _____

CLASS _____

SKILL OR CONCEPT	LEARNING ACTIVITIES	TEACHING POINTS	TIME

Note. From *Badminton: A Structures of Knowledge Approach* (p. 95) by J.N. Vickers and D. Brecht, 1987, Calgary, AB: University Printing Services. Copyright 1987 by Joan N. Vickers. Reprinted by permission.

References

Goc-Karp, G., & Zakrajsek, D.B. (1987). Planning for learning: Theory into practice. *Journal of Teaching in Physical Education*, **6**(4), 377-392.

Housner, L.D., & Griffey, D.C. (1985). Teacher cognition: Differences in planning and interactive decision making between experienced and inexperienced teachers. *Research Quarterly for Exercise and Sport*, **56**(1), 45-53.

Imwold, C.H., & Hoffman, S.J. (1983). Visual recognition of a gymnastic skill by experienced and inexperienced instructors. *Research Quarterly for Exercise and Sport*, **54**(2), 149-155.

Suggested Readings

American Red Cross. (1981). *Swimming and aquatics safety*. Washington, DC: Author.

YMCA Progressive Swimming Program Instructor's Guide. (1986). Champaign, IL: Human Kinetics.

About the Author

David G. Thomas has been a swimming teacher and coach since 1948, when he became a water safety field representative for the American National Red Cross. In 1955 he became swimming coach and director of aquatics at Berea High School, Berea, Ohio. Eight years later he moved to the State University of New York at Binghamton, where he was director of aquatics and swimming coach until retiring as professor emeritus in 1985.

Thomas gained nationwide prominence in 1972 by producing a textbook, a teaching guide, exams, and visual aids for training swimming pool operators. The *Swimming Pool Operators Handbook* and the other materials were published by the National Swimming Pool Foundation as the basis for their Certified Pool Operators program.

Thomas has published many articles on aquatic subjects and is a contributing author to several books on swimming pool design and operation. He has been writing extensively since retirement, with his most recent book being *Competitive Swimming Management* (Leisure Press, 1988). Soon to be released is *Professional Aquatic Management*, co-authored with Robert Clayton (Leisure Press, 1989). Self-employed as a consultant in aquatics and pool design and operation, Thomas lives with his wife, Virginia, in Anderson, SC. He enjoys scuba diving and boating in his leisure time and swims a mile or more each day for fitness.